✳ domestic arts for crafty girls

MATERIAL WORLD

Home Décor Projects
for the Fabric Obsessed

ROCKPORT

BEVERLY MASSACHUSETTS

* domestic arts for crafty girls

MATERIAL WORLD

Home Décor Projects
for the Fabric Obsessed

Cat Wei

as seen on DIY Network's
Material Girls

QUARRY BOOKS

First published in the United States of America by
Quarry Books, a member of
Quayside Publishing Group
100 Cummings Center
Suite 406-L
Beverly, Massachusetts 01915-6101
Telephone: (978) 282-9590
Fax: (978) 283-2742
www.quarrybooks.com

Library of Congress Cataloging-in-Publication Data
Wei, Catherine.
   Material world : home décor projects for the fabric obsessed /
Catherine Wei.
       p. cm. — (Domestic arts for crafty girls)
   ISBN 1-59253-358-2 (pbk.)
   1. Sewing. 2. Household linens. 3. House furnishings. I. Title.
TT703.W45 2007
646.4—dc22

                                                   2007004534
                                                         CIP

Material World contains a variety of design tips and suggestions. While caution was taken to give safe recommendations, it is imperative to use responsible judgment regarding the safe execution of these projects. Neither the author, Catherine Wei, nor the Publisher, Quayside Publishing Group, accepts liability for any mental, financial, or physical harm that arises from following the advice, techniques, and procedures in this book.

ISBN-13: 978-1-59253-358-9
ISBN-10: 1-59253-358-2

10 9 8 7 6 5 4 3 2 1

Design: Stephen Gleason Design
Photography: Allan Penn and Creative Publishing international
Cover image: Allan Penn
Cover fabric: Amy Butler, Belle Gothic Rose Burgundy
All illustrations by Michael Wanke except pages 34, 35, 145 by Lainé Roundy
Technical editing by Beth Baumgartel and Patricia Harste

Printed in China

For my Mom
and Dad

page 10

page 42

page 124

Contents

page 28

page 80

page 18

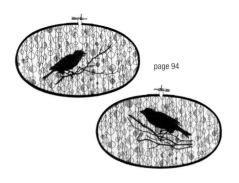
page 94

page 22

page 14

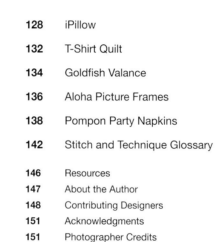
page 26

page 96

The Aesthetics of Textiles

As a TV design-show veteran, I'm lucky to have participated in three fun and exciting home shows. The fast pace of these shows exposed me to a wide variety of new experiences. My usual challenge was to design something fresh for an outdated room. It was always a client I had never met, a town I had never been to, and a few hours working with limited resources. Time after time, I found myself gravitating toward fabric as the solution to every design dilemma. If I developed designer's block, lo and behold, fabric came to the rescue. I often found a one-of-a-kind fabric to serve as foundation for the room's design.

Fabric, as a design tool, has the ability to transform space and define the character and mood of a room. Stimulating colors, sensuous textures, and playful patterns have the power to captivate and inspire. Visit a fabric design center or warehouse, and you'll discover that the combinations of color, pattern, and texture are capable of giving you a visual headache! Fabric is undeniably versatile as a design medium. It is pliable and can be molded to take the shape of a chair, stiffened to stand as a room screen, or draped over a curtain rod to filter light and blow with the wind.

Think of fabric as the new paint: just as a fresh coat rejuvenates a room, visual patterns and crisp fabrics can breathe life into even the most neglected spaces. Fabric can serve many purposes and solve a plethora of design problems, both decorative and functional. Your home and your environment are an extension of your body and soul, and wear many different outfits. So, dress it up! Fabric can take you on a visual and tactile journey without ever leaving home. *Material World* will help you revitalize the rooms in your home, one project at a time! Search the Internet or visit fabric stores to locate many of the same and/or similar fabrics shown on these pages, or choose your own fabrics, ones that reflect your style and personality. Many of our designers chose basics, such as burlap, linen, and painter's canvas, which are simple to customize and readily available.

About Inspiration

Inspiration is what makes a designer tick. Look for it in everyday objects, trips around the block, or travels to other countries. It can come from, but is not limited to, nature, art, architecture, world cultures, your memories, or that shabby lamp your grandmother gave you. Whether it is a literal translation or something more abstract, inspiration is motivating: a muse that formulates the big idea. The challenge is to embrace what inspires you and translate it into something beautiful for your home. Open your eyes, or as my Taiwanese father likes to say, "*abre sus ojos.*"

For me, inspiration is going to our beach house every summer to escape the hectic city pace or visiting my parents in the house in which I grew up. My experiences and memories inspire me and are reborn in many of the items that I create. The boundless energy of my dog Duke running down the beach, my mother at her sewing machine, and my wedding by the ocean in Hawaii, are just a few fond memories that have inspired me.

If you're at a loss about where to start, pull tear sheets from your favorite home design magazines (or any other printed matter) and begin analyzing them. It's always a surprise to my clients when I find a recurring theme in their choices, such as pumpkin orange or animal prints, although they've assured me that they prefer a palette of neutral colors, conveying just the opposite. This exercise will unearth a decorating style, which can then be translated into something physical, like a window treatment, a side table, or even a piece of art.

Material World will give you the tools you need to create beautiful objects for your home (Am I sounding like an infomercial yet?). It's chock full of projects for the beginner as well as the seasoned sewer. Start with a level one project. You'll be delighted when you feel the same satisfaction that you felt when you traced your hand and made a construction paper turkey in kindergarten. Several projects in this book start with ready-made things that merely require a little customizing (like the Mod-ern Tasseled Shade), or begin with something you already own that you will be asked to retro-fit (such as the Poolside Resort Director's Chair).

Do good things for your home and in turn your soul, with a do-it-yourself project that sparks your creative spirit. You'll find it's cheaper than a therapist and far more productive! Beautify your home with imaginative objects and decorative ideas…pleasant rooms make for pleasant people!

Do-It-Yourself

Material World is a guidebook of inspirational home décor projects, created by a variety of talented designers. The backgrounds of the contributors run the gamut. They include three architects, a fashion photographer, a professional seamstress, a handbag designer, an online notions boutique owner, an art director, a graphic design couple, a knitting guru, a fashion magazine editor, several clothing and textile designers, and a handful of multimedia artists.

Vintage Button Pillows

Everyone has a collection of buttons stashed somewhere. Get them out of the jar and showcase them on a novel, vintage button pillow.

When my mother and I sat down to work on this set of pillows, I started with an intriguing collection of vintage buttons from an online source. My mother jumped up, ran to her room, and dragged out a worn hatbox, from a now-defunct department store. The hatbox was filled with miscellaneous treasures, including packs of mint-condition and single "antique" buttons that prompted fond childhood memories. As I sewed a deep purple velvet button onto my pillow, I was reminded of the velvet coat my mother made in the late 1970s (it was my favorite jacket on her). Next, I discovered a red and black ladybug button, a leftover from the dress my mother made for me when I was in grade school!

My 4" x 6" (10.2 x 15.2 cm) pillow captured the preciousness of the buttons. Mom's 4½" x 9" (11.4 x 22.9 cm) pillow was a bit more ambitious since it required more patience and more buttons. Use flax-colored, medium-to heavy-weight linen, cotton, or muslin broadcloth to give the pillow vintage character. The fabric must be stiff enough to hold the weight of the buttons. Include a few mother-of-pearl buttons; they have a wonderfully authentic antique sheen.

Vintage buttons, found at a flea market, reflect the art and fashion of time gone by.

Instructions:

1. Cut two pieces of fabric 5" x 7" (12.7 x 17.8 cm) for the small pillow, or 7"x 9" (17.8 x 22.9 cm) for the large pillow.

2. With right sides together, sew the pieces with a ½" (1.3 cm) seam allowance around the perimeter. Leave a 4" (10.2 cm) opening in one long edge. Turn the pillow right side out.

3. Fold the unstitched edges ½" (1.3 cm) to the inside and press.

4. Divide the buttons into groups by size: small, medium, and large.

5. Sew the buttons onto one of the fabric pieces; do not sew through both, or you won't be able to stuff the pillow. Use colorful threads to sew on the neutral-color buttons and complementary threads to sew on the colorful buttons. Sew on the large buttons first, spacing them evenly over the pillow front. Fill in the large spaces with the medium buttons and the small spaces with the small buttons, spacing them as close to one another as possible, so they lay flat.

6. Lightly stuff the pillow with fiberfill. Slipstitch the opening closed (See Slipstitch, page 142).

Tip: I found hotel mini sewing kits to be very helpful for this project; eight prestrung needles with different color threads!

Tools:

❀ Hand sewing needle
❀ Iron and ironing board
❀ Ruler
❀ Scissors
❀ Sewing machine

Materials:

❀ 14" (35.6 cm) square of medium-weight linen, cotton, or muslin
❀ Generous handful of vintage buttons (approximately 60 for the small pillow and 90 for the large pillow)
❀ Contrasting threads
❀ Polyester fiberfill

Oilcloth Nesting Tables

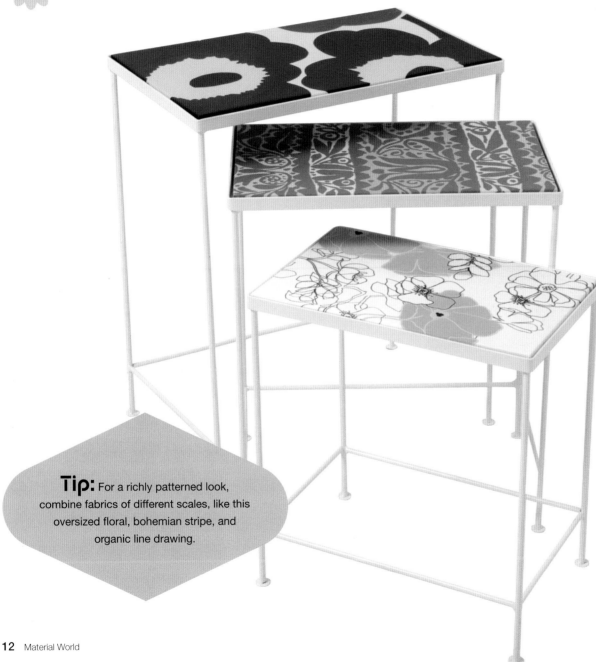

Tip: For a richly patterned look, combine fabrics of different scales, like this oversized floral, bohemian stripe, and organic line drawing.

Tools:

* Newspaper or other floor protection
* Power drill fitted with ⅛" (3 mm) drill bit (optional)
* Rag
* Sandpaper, #100 and #220
* Screwdriver (optional)
* Staple gun and staples
* Tack cloth
* Two 1" (2.5 cm) flat paintbrushes

Materials:

* Three metal nesting tables with framed tops and removable inserts
* Gel rust remover, such as Naval Jelly
* White spray primer for metal, such as Rust-Oleum
* White semi-gloss or high-gloss enamel paint for metal
* Three squares of ½" (1.3 cm) -thick MDF (medium density fiberboard) cut ⅛" (3 mm) smaller on all sides than the framed tops of the tables (use the original inserts if undamaged)
* Three squares of oilcloth cut 2" (5.1 cm) larger on all sides than the inserts (see Resources, page 146)
* Twelve ⅜" (1 cm) -long #4 wood screws (optional)

Wooden Russian nesting dolls are called *matryoshka*, a name derived from the Latin root mater, meaning "mother." The dolls depict characters from everyday life, such as peasant girls, brides, and historical persons. Matryoshka range in size from 3" to 14" (7.5 to 35.5 cm), and contain from three to twenty dolls that fit comfortably within one other and within the largest doll. Combined, these dolls are secretively simple; separated, they are charming individual pieces of art, each one painted by hand with intricate details and bright colors on a consistent background.

I picked up this trio of mangy-looking, metal nesting tables at a tag sale around the corner from my parent's house for ten bucks. Loading them into the back of my husband's truck, I heard myself telling him, "I'll pay you back, I promise." Joel rolled his eyes, and I knew he was thinking he'd hear me beg for help to refinish them. His contractor knowledge did come in handy when he prescribed Naval Jelly (which I call orange marmalade), a secret potion (that is actually orange) for dissolving rust. I decided to paint the tables white, because their shape reminded me of the sophisticated outdoor furniture designed by Richard Schultz, like the kind you might find at a ritzy hotel pool area in Miami. The fabric inserts are made of colorful oilcloth, a water-resistant fabric with a durable coating. Oilcloth has a smooth finish, so when it's stretched taut it seems that the fabric's pattern has been painted on, much like the dolls'.

The following process works for any metal table frame with a removable top that is begging for a second chance. Scour your local flea market or hit those tag sales.

Russian *matryoshka* nesting dolls are a charmingly unique combination of art and toy.

Instructions:

1. Sand the tables with #100 sandpaper to remove the heaviest rust. Wipe clean with the rag.

2. Following the manufacturer's instructions, use a paintbrush to apply the gel rust remover to all sides and leave it on for the recommended length of time. Rinse thoroughly with water and let dry.

3. Spray tables with the primer and let dry.

4. Sand lightly with the #220 sandpaper. Wipe clean with the tack cloth.

5. Use the other paintbrush to apply two coats of enamel paint. Allow the paint to dry thoroughly after each coat.

6. For each insert, place an oilcloth square face down and then center the new or original insert on top of it.

7. Staple one side of the oilcloth to the insert, stapling to within 2" (5.1 cm) of the corners. Then staple the side opposite, keeping the fabric taut. Repeat for the last two sides.

8. At each corner, fold the oilcloth in two inverted pleats, and then staple the folds to secure. Repeat at each corner, and then trim the oilcloth that extends beyond the staples. (See How to Staple a Corner Fold, page 144.)

9. Center the inserts in the framed tops.

(OPTIONAL) If there are screw holes in the tabletops, fasten the inserts from underneath with screws. To do this, mark the position of the screw holes on the underside of each insert. At each mark, drill ¼" (6 mm) -deep pilot holes. Secure screws through the holes in the table and into the pilot holes, using the screwdriver.

Do you want to update that set of rusty tables in the garage? A collage of oilcloth fabrics adds playful personality to a modern furniture silhouette.

Tomato Floor Pillow

When a vegetable becomes a floor cushion...you can't eat it, but you can plant yourself on it!

Sitting at the picnic table and eating a summer salad at our beach house, I began to have visions of the tomatoes that went into the salad. The heirloom tomatoes, bought fresh from the roadside farmer's stand, are awesome. Every heirloom tomato variety has a story. Often the stories are handed down from one generation to another, stretching back hundreds of years. Each one is unique in shape and color, wildly hexagonal with complicated reds, oranges, yellows, or greens. This musing inspired the idea for our tomato floor pillow. The center is tufted on the top and bottom, as if it were once connected to a vine. The finished size of the pillow is 30" (76.2 cm) in diameter x 12" (30.5 cm) high.

Tools:

❁ Craft paper, 19" x 21" (48.3 x 53.3 cm)
❁ Hand sewing needle
❁ Iron and ironing board
❁ Pencil
❁ Ruler
❁ Scissors
❁ Sewing machine
❁ Straight pins
❁ Straight upholstery needle, 10" (25.4 cm)

Materials:

❁ 3 yards (2.75 m) of 54" (137 cm) -wide medium-weight cotton upholstery fabric
❁ 10" (25.4 cm) square medium-weight green silk
❁ Two size 75 (1⅞" [4.8 cm]) self-cover buttons
❁ Ten 12 oz. (342.8 g) bags polyester fiberfill
❁ Matching thread
❁ Heavy cotton yarn to match green silk

The oldest tomato, known as the "Moneymaker," is an English variety between 250 and 300 years old!

Tip: The button application is formed by a process called tufting. See the illustration on page 17 for guidance.

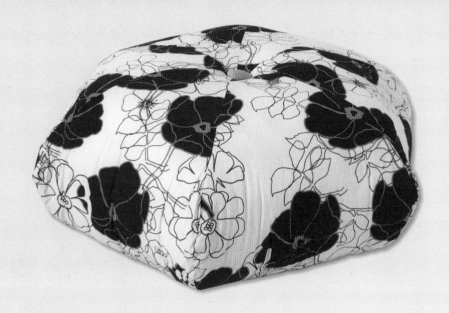

Instructions:

1. Using a pencil and ruler, measure and mark the center of 21" (53.3 cm) top edge of craft paper. On 21" (53.3 cm) bottom edge, measure and mark 1" (2.5 cm) in from each side edge. Connect the center top mark to each of the bottom marks to form a triangle that's 19" (48.3 cm) tall and 19" (48.3 cm) wide at the base. Measure and mark 1" (2.5 cm) down from both the top left and top right corners. Draw a line connecting these marks. Cut along this line to remove the top (sharp point) of the pattern. Cut along the two remaining lines to form the pattern.

Step 1

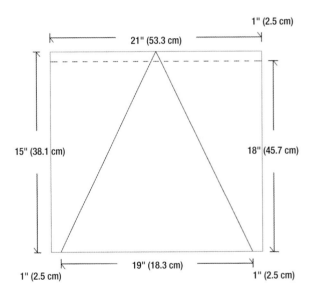

2. Fold fabric in half lengthwise, so right sides are facing. Pin the pattern to fabric so 19" (48.3 cm) base is on the fold. Cut out. Working in the same manner, cut out five more pieces.

3. Open up the fabric pieces and stack two sets of three pieces. Trim off the sharp points on each side where the fabric was folded, to soften the edges. (See illustration, below.)

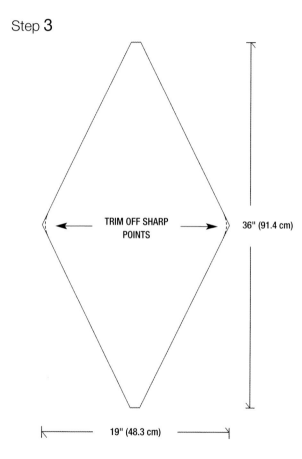

Step 3

← TRIM OFF SHARP POINTS →

36" (91.4 cm)

19" (48.3 cm)

4. Pin two pieces together along one long edge so right sides are facing.

5. Sew five pairs of seams together, using a ½" (1.3 cm) seam allowance. Sew the last seam, leaving a 10" (25.4 cm) opening between the center of the pillow and the outside edge. Clip seams around corners. Press the seams open. Turn right side out.

6. Stuff the pillow firmly with the fiberfill. Slipstitch (See Slipstitch, page 142) the opening closed.

7. Cover the buttons with silk, following the package directions.

8. To tuft the pillow, cut a 25" (63.5 cm) length of cotton yarn. Tie one end of the yarn securely to the shank of one button. Thread the opposite end of the yarn into the upholstery needle. Insert the needle through the center of the pillow top, out the center of the pillow back, then through the shank of the remaining button. Pull the yarn tight to tuft, and then knot securely under the button shank.

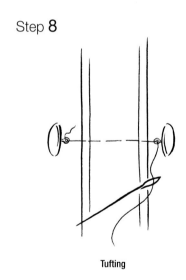

Step 8

Tufting

Warhol Fabric Art

Andy Warhol produced a series of silk-screened portraits by transferring photographed images to canvas. His famed celebrity portraits included Marilyn Monroe, Elvis Presley, Jacqueline Kennedy, and Mao Zedong. He also duplicated images of mass-produced commercial products such as Campbell's soup cans and Brillo boxes. Warhol's art was a commentary on the marketing of celebrities as consumer products.

OK, the fabric-covered-canvas-as-wall-art is old news, so we've added a new twist; and just in case you are afraid to fire up the staple gun, we've included simple instructions to get you started. Any square canvas dimension will work to create this Warhol inspired "grid," you just need four of them. Find a textile print that comes in several vibrant colorways. The end product will be a four-square grid of color and pattern, reminiscent of art from the most recognized pop-artist icon of the modern age. By displaying one fabric pattern in four different colors, you create a sophisticated, substantially sized piece of art...perfect filler for those blank white walls!

Fabric pop art is inspired by the late artist Andy Warhol's many silk-screened personalities.

Bring pop culture to a wall near you!

Tools:

❋ Four nails for hanging
❋ Hammer
❋ Ruler
❋ Scissors
❋ Staple gun and staples

Materials:

❋ Four 24" x 24" (61 x 61 cm) prestretched artist canvases
❋ Four 30" (76.2 cm) squares of print fabric in four colorways
❋ Four 2" (5.1 cm) sawtooth picture hangers with enclosed brads

Instructions:

1. Cut the four pieces of fabric so that each has the same image. Press the edge ½" (1.3 cm) to the wrong side all the way around.

2. Lay the fabric face down and position the canvas on top of it.

3. Staple one side of the fabric to the canvas stretcher strip. Staple to within 2" (5.1 cm) of the corners. Then staple the side opposite. Keep the fabric taut without distorting the image.

4. Repeat for the last two sides.

5. At each corner, fold the fabric in two inverted pleats, then staple the folds on the back of the canvas to secure (See How to Staple a Corner Fold on page 144). Repeat at each corner, and then trim away excess fabric that extends beyond the staples.

6. Nail a sawtooth hanger at the center top of the back of the canvas.

7. Repeat for the remaining three canvases.

8. Hang the fabric art 2" (5.1 cm) apart on the wall to form a grid.

2

Candy-Coated Toile Bench

Fact: *Toile*, which means "cloth" in French, originated as a decorating fabric in the 1800s. It usually consists of a main color as the background with a second color as the line drawing.

Toile has been a classic textile design for as long as anyone can remember, so we thought it would be cool to update it with youthful color on a traditional piece of furniture.

My business partner (or work spouse as I like to call him) and I were working in a palatial Fifth Avenue apartment overlooking Central Park for a very important client. On a typical site visit we were left unsupervised. As we wandered through the kitchen, a Plexiglas box, etched with "For Noshers Only," caught my eye. An assortment of gourmet candy jelly beans with exotic names like "buttered popcorn" and "tutti fruitti" teased our grumbling bellies. Our professionalism was overtaken by sweet temptation. Our client quickly busted us, with our hands quite literally in the candy jar! Although our sugar snack party was interrupted, the dots of colors and playful shapes remained in my memory and provided the inspiration for this project.

Candy colors are so enticing; they make us forget how old we are (or where we are, as in our case). In my vivid memory, the white candy wrappers created the borders for the bright colored jellybeans to fill. Black-and-white toile provides the perfect outline for colorful candy. By using candy-colored tapestry threads, we added youth to a classic fabric and a traditional furniture shape. If you remember the rules of your kindergarten coloring books, then this project will be a cinch, whether or not you choose to stay within the lines.

A kaleidoscope of colorful, candy jelly beans, separated by white dividers, are sweet temptations.

Tools:

* Crewel embroidery needle
* Dressmaker's scissors
* Embroidery scissors
* Iron and ironing board
* Paintbrushes (2)
* Pins
* Sandpaper, #120 and #220
* Screwdriver
* Staple gun and staples
* Tack cloth

Materials:

* Wooden bench or footstool with removable upholstered seat or top
* 1 yard (1 m) 54" (137.1 cm) -wide toile fabric
* Six or more candy-color shades of tapestry wool or six-strand embroidery floss
* White all-purpose primer
* Bright red semi-gloss acrylic paint

Instructions:

1. Remove the seat (or the top). Use the screwdriver to remove the staples that secure the old fabric cover. Press the old cover to remove wrinkles.

2. Using the old cover as a pattern, position it over the desired area of the fabric. Pin in place, and then cut the new fabric 1" (2.5 cm) larger all around than the old fabric. Choose the design details, such as birds, trees, hats, and clothing, in the fabric pattern to "color in" with embroidery stitches.

3. Embroider the fabric details, using one strand of tapestry yarn, or all six strands of embroidery floss. Use the photograph for inspiration and a variety of stitches to create interesting textures. Make sure to distribute the colors to create a balanced composition. (For stitch instructions, see pages 142–144.)

4. Sand the bench (or the footstool) using the #120 sandpaper, then the #220. Wipe clean with the tack cloth.

5. Apply one to two coats of the primer, following the label directions. Let dry thoroughly. Sand with the #220 sandpaper. Wipe clean with the tack cloth.

6. Apply two or three coats of the acrylic paint, allowing each coat to dry thoroughly before applying the next coat. For the best results, lightly sand between coats, using the #220 sandpaper, and wipe clean with the tack cloth.

7. Lay the embroidered fabric face down and position the seat (or the top) face down on it.

8. Staple one long side of the fabric to the wrong side of the seat (or top), to within 2" (5.1 cm) of the corners. Then staple the side opposite, keeping the fabric taut.

9. Repeat for the last two short sides.

10. At each corner, fold the fabric in two inverted pleats, and then staple the folds to secure. (See How to Staple a Corner Fold, page 144.) Repeat at each corner, and trim away excess fabric that extends beyond the staples.

11. Reattach the newly covered seat (or top) to the bench or footstool.

2

Poolside Resort Director's Chair

Tip: If you plan to keep your chair outdoors, use weather-resistant fabric made with solution-dyed acrylic yarns that make it stain and fade resistant, and mildew proof.

Watch the pool boys from this cool chair.

The resort collection of any fashion (or home) designer is certain to include the colors of the white beaches and blue ocean tides, reminiscent of the spectacular scenery in Santorini, Greece. Santorini is a tiny volcanic island in the Aegean Sea. The town of Oia clings to the volcanic hills with crisp, white stucco structures, cave dwellings, and domed churches, which are interspersed with turquoise swimming pools. This man-made landscape effortlessly enhances the richness of the sea and the wispy blue hues of the sky. The contrast between the whites and blues is breathtaking, and it serves as inspiration for our director's chair, made with exotic ikat fabric. Picture yourself wearing your favorite Jackie O sunglasses and white linen caftan, relaxing in this fabulous chair at home, and you'll think you're still on vacation.

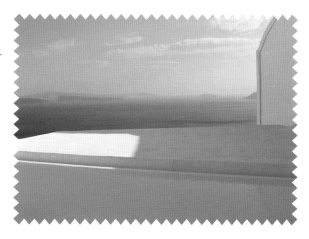

Bring home the memories of Santorini, Greece: the landscape, the ocean, and the amazing architecture.

Tools:

❀ Iron & ironing board
❀ Masking tape
❀ Pins
❀ Press cloth
❀ Quilter's basting spray
❀ Ruler
❀ Scissors
❀ Seam ripper
❀ Sewing machine with overlock stitch capability
❀ Tape measure

Materials:

❀ Director's chair with white frame and existing canvas seat and back
❀ 2 yards (2 m) lightweight cotton canvas or broadcloth (equal to the weight of the existing cover when doubled)
❀ Matching heavy-duty thread

Instructions:

1. Remove the seat and back from the chair and use them as patterns to cut the new fabric. Remove the dowel stick guides from the seat. Using the seam ripper, open up all seams and hems. Leave all serged edges intact. Press, using a damp press cloth to remove creases and fold lines.

2. Measure across the width of the seat, and pin-mark the center at top and bottom edges. Repeat for the back of the chair.

3. Cut the new fabric in half so you have two 1-yard (1 m) pieces. Place one of the fabric pieces wrong side up on your work surface. Spray the wrong side with basting spray. Place the corresponding piece, right side up, on top, centering or aligning the design. Smooth, using firm pressure, to adhere the fabric pieces together.

4. Pin the seat and back patterns to the double layer of fabric, using the pin marks to center them on the design. Cut out. Indicate the wrong side of each piece with a square of masking tape.

5. For the seat, finish the short side edges with an overlock stitch. Turn the long top edge ⅛" (3 mm) to the wrong side. Press. Turn the same edge ⅜" (1 cm) to the wrong side. Press. With the wrong side facing up, topstitch close to the inner folded edge. Repeat on the long bottom edge.

6. For the dowel guide pocket, turn one short side edge ⅞" (2.2 cm) to the wrong side. With the wrong side facing up, topstitch ¼" (6 mm) from the overlock-stitched edge. Repeat on the opposite short edge. Remove the masking tape square.

7. For the back, turn the long top edge ¼" (6 mm) to the wrong side. Press. Turn the same edge ⁷⁄₁₆" (1.1 cm) to the wrong side. Press. With the wrong side facing up, topstitch close to inner folded edge. Repeat on the long bottom edge.

8. For the back support pocket, turn one short side edge ½" (1.3 cm) to the wrong side. Press. Turn the same edge 2¾" (7 cm) to the wrong side. Press. With the wrong side facing up, and sewing across the entire width of the back, topstitch close to inner folded edge, Stitch again, over previous stitching to reinforce the seam. Topstitch again ¼" (6 mm) from previous topstitching. Repeat, on the opposite short side edge. Remove the masking tape square.

9. To reassemble the chair, insert dowel stick guides into pockets, then slide seat into chair frame. Slip back support pockets onto back supports, then open up chair and lock in place.

Deluxe Duvet

Tools:

* Disappearing-ink fabric pen
* Hand sewing needle
* Iron and ironing board
* Pins
* Ruler
* Scissors
* Seam ripper
* Sewing machine with buttonhole capability
* Tape measure

Materials:

* Queen sheet set (flat sheet, fitted sheet, and two pillowcases) in a solid color
* King flat sheet in a floral print
* 2½ yards (2.5 m) ½" (13 mm) -wide cotton twill tape (for optional ties)
* Three ⅝" (16 mm) buttons
* Matching sewing threads

A rustic, red barn exudes Americana.

Create a designer duvet set from a couple of bed sheets!

Tip: Believe it or not, you will still have leftover floral fabric. Use the flowers in the pattern as an appliqué. (See instructions for Recycled Denim Headboard Slipcover on page 72.)

Duvets always cost an arm and a leg, and we've all wondered why! Isn't it the same amount of material as a couple of bed sheets? It most certainly is, so we decided to take bed sheets and transform them into a deluxe duvet, complete with upgraded pillowcases.

Shop your local discount store for name-brand designer sheets. For a double- or queen-size duvet, you'll need a solid-color, queen-size sheet set with pillow cases and a patterned, king-size flat sheet. Inspired by sophisticated Americana country style, I shopped and found this poppy red floral pattern king sheet and faded denim queen set. Set the fitted queen sheet aside and use it to dress the bed. The floral is the focal fabric for the top of the duvet, and the flat, faded denim sheet will be the bottom of duvet. After you trim the king sheet to fit a queen-size duvet, you will have extra patterned fabric to embellish the edges of the two pillowcases. I can see it now...on the bed of the coveted guest room in your fabulous country cottage.

Instructions:

FOR DUVET COVER:

1. Press the sheets. Place the king flat sheet right side up on the floor, so the wide top hem of the sheet is at the top. Place the queen flat sheet wrong side up on top of the king flat sheet, so the wide top hems and the right side edges are even. Smooth the sheets and pin the edges together.

2. Using the ruler and the fabric marker, measure and mark on the king sheet, 1½" (3.8 cm) from the bottom and the left side edges of the queen sheet. Cut the excess fabric from the king sheet along the markings. Unpin the sheets.

3. Turn the left side edge of the king sheet ¾" (1.9 cm) to the wrong side twice. Press, and topstitch near the inner folded edge. Repeat along the bottom edge.

4. Pin the sheets together so the wrong sides are facing, the wide top hems are together, and all edges are even. Sew the side and bottom seams, just inside the hem stitching lines.

5. At the top open edge, measure and pin-mark 29" (73.7 cm) in from each side edge and 2" (5.1 cm) down from the top edges.

6. Using the 2" (5.1 cm) seam allowance, sew the top edges together from the side edge to the pin marks, leaving the center open. Backstitch. Turn the cover right side out and press.

7. For the optional ties, to hold the duvet inside the duvet cover, cut the twill tape into eight equal lengths. Pin the end of one tie to the seam allowance in one inside corner of the duvet cover, and stitch forward and backward a few times to secure it. Repeat for the three remaining corners. For the duvet, you can either sew the ties as for the cover, or pin them in place with safety pins.

8. With the floral print side facing, measure and pin-mark the placement of two button holes 7½" (19.1 cm) from each edge of the opening. Measure and pin-mark for one buttonhole in the center of the opening.

9. Working ¼" (6 mm) from the edge, make a ⅝" (1.6 cm) vertical buttonhole at each pin mark through the floral fabric only. Carefully, cut open the buttonholes.

10. Bring the open top edges together and pin. Use the fabric marker to make a mark in the center of each buttonhole for button placement.

11. With thread doubled, sew the buttons through the 2" (5.1 cm) -wide flange (formed by the seam allowance). The buttoned opening is now the bottom of the duvet cover.

FOR PILLOWCASES:

1. Use the seam ripper to open the seams of the pillowcases. Press the pillowcases flat.

2. For each pillowcase, cut a 7" x 42" (17.8 x 106.7 cm) strip from the leftover king sheet. Press ½" (1.3 cm) to the wrong side along one long edge.

3. With right sides together, place the fabric strip so the unpressed, long raw edge is ½" (1.3 cm) above the pillowcase hem stitching 4½" (11.4 cm) from the top edge. The side edges align. Machine baste.

4. Turn the pillowcase to the wrong side and sew through all layers just below the existing hem stitching. Trim side edges if necessary. Remove basting stitches.

5. Fold the strip to the right side (over the existing pillowcase hem) and press.

6. Fold the top edge of the fabric strip over the pillowcase edge and topstitch it in place, close to the pressed edge.

7. Re-sew the pillowcase across the bottom and up the side with right sides together. Turn right side out and press.

Ruched Lace Lampshade

Frills and lace can be naughty or nice, and this ruched lampshade is really nice...and it's easy!

Lampshades vary in shape and size, but this loose and lacy version is very forgiving. Don't worry about perfect measurements or using too much lace (sounds like a dream, doesn't it?) because extra lace and a little imperfection only add to the fullness of the ruffles. Top the shade with embellishments, such as old costume jewelry, or fancy feathers glued front and center for retro movie-star glamour. Picture this romantic light fixture in your boudoir, with you wearing your sexiest pair of lace panties and bask in the de-light cast by both!

Ruffled panties are pretty in pink.

Tools:

❀ Hand sewing needle
❀ Hot glue gun and glue sticks
❀ Iron and ironing board
❀ Paper, 8" x 19" (20.3 x 48.3 cm)
❀ Pencil
❀ Pins
❀ Press cloth
❀ Scissors
❀ Sewing machine
❀ Yardstick

Materials:

❀ Bell-shaped lampshade with six ribs (white) 11" (27.9 cm) diameter at the base x 9" (22.9 cm) high
❀ Lamp base with harp, sized to fit shade
❀ ¾ yard (61 cm) 54" (137.1 cm) -wide pink lace fabric
❀ 3½ yards (3.2 m) ½" (13 mm) -wide ribbon
❀ 1 yard (1 m) ⅜" (10 mm) ball trim
❀ Matching thread
❀ Embellishments such as costume jewelry, feathers, and crocheted or lace appliqués

Instructions:

1. Draw a 1" (2.5 cm) grid on the piece of paper. See instructions, page 145.

2. Copy the half pattern for the lampshade panel, line-for-line, onto the grid. The seam allowances are included in the pattern. Cut out the pattern. (See Templates, page 154.)

3. Fold the lace fabric in half. Position the pattern so the dashed line is on the fold of the fabric. Pin, and then cut out. Repeat for five more panels.

4. With the right sides together, and a ½" (1.3 cm) seam allowance, sew the panels together along the long edges to make a continuous cover. Press the seams open, using the press cloth. Turn the top and bottom edges ½" (1.3 cm) to the wrong side, sew close to the fold, then press.

5. Sew gathering stitches along each vertical panel seam. Pull the gathering threads so the panel seams are 9" (22.9 cm) long. Distribute the gathers evenly, then machine stitch directly over the seams (See Stitch in the Ditch, on page 144). Remove the gathering threads.

6. Sew two rows of gathering stitches across the top and bottom edges. Place the lace cover back on the shade. Pull the threads and adjust the gathers so the seams align with the ribs on the shade. Remove the lace cover from the shade and machine stitch, close to the fold, to secure the gathers. Remove the gathering threads.

7. Place the lace cover on the shade. Use the hot glue gun to adhere the fabric seams to the ribs on the shade. Hot glue the top and bottom edges of the lace cover to the shade.

8. Hot glue the ball trim to the inside bottom edge of the shade, overlapping the ends. Hot glue the embellishments to the center front of the shade.

9. Cut ribbon into six 21" (53.3 cm) lengths. Tie each into a bow and hot glue to the bottom of the shade at each of the seams.

DIFFICULTY RATING

3

Patchwork Taxidermy Animal Rug

Crazy-quilted patchwork and an animal silhouette conjure up images of a bearskin rug in front of the fireplace at a cozy Rocky Mountain ski lodge. Use your favorite combination of color and pattern for a quilt that you can lay on the floor as a rug, hang on the wall as a tapestry, or throw across the foot of a bed or worn leather armchair as a blanket. Regardless of where it ends up, it is sure to be a conversation piece!

Cozy up your home with a politically correct animal skin rug, one that is made out of colorful patchwork squares, quilted into the shape of a friendly bear!

Fuzzy Wuzzy was a bear

Tip: Make a mini version for your pup, so he can snuggle with it in his new Twig Dog Bed. Turn to page 32for instructions on how to make that bed!

Tools:

❋ Clear tape
❋ Hand sewing needle
❋ Iron and ironing board
❋ Pins
❋ Sewing machine
❋ Scissors
❋ Two 26" x 50" (66 x 127 cm) pieces of paper
❋ Yardstick

Materials:

❋ Large scraps of coordinating medium-weight fabrics
❋ 1⅓ yards (1.3 m) 45" (114.3 cm) -wide muslin for the interfacing
❋ 1¼ yards (1.25 m) 54" (137.2 cm) -wide brocade for the backing
❋ Small amount of fiberfill

Instructions:

1. Use the yardstick to draw a 2" (5.1 cm) grid on one 26" x 50" (66 x 127 cm) piece of paper. Set the other piece aside.

2. Copy the half pattern for the rug (See page 155), line-for-line, onto the grid. (See guide drawing and instructions, page 145) Add ½" (1.3 cm) seam allowance to all edges except the dashed line. Cut the pattern along the dashed line. Tape the dashed line to the 50" (127 cm) edge of the remaining piece of paper. Fold along the dashed line and cut out the pattern through both layers. Unfold the paper to make the complete bear-shaped pattern.

3. Use a photocopier to enlarge the ear and tail patterns at 300%. (See Templates, page 155.) Cut out for the patterns.

4. Prewash and press all the fabrics. The widest dimension of the muslin becomes the width of the rug.

5. Begin the front patchwork fabric: Cut a five-sided piece of decorative fabric and pin it, right side up, in the center of the muslin. Stitch one edge using a ³⁄₁₆" (0.5 cm) seam.

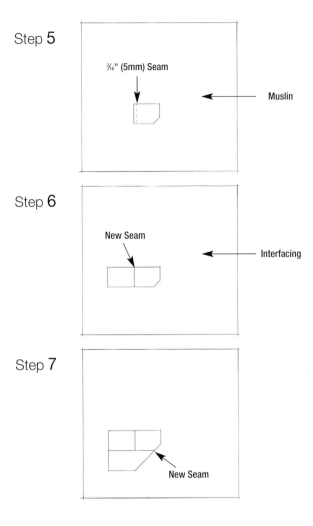

Muslin and patchwork pieces

6. Cut a rectangle of fabric the same height as the first piece. Place it right side down on the first piece, matching the same height edges. With a ¼" (6 mm) seam, stitch through both pieces of decorator fabric and the muslin backing. Unfold the second piece so it is right side up, and press the seam. It is crucial to be neat and to press all pieces flat as you work, to avoid puckers later.

7. Repeat step 6, cutting and adding pieces to all sides of the growing rectangle, until the muslin is covered with patchwork. Every piece you add does not have to be the same height as the previous piece; shorter pieces result in more patchwork. Refer to the photograph.

8. Use the rug pattern to cut out the patchwork front. Sew zigzag stitches ¼" (6 mm) from the perimeter to attach the edges of the patchwork to the muslin.

9. Use the rug pattern to cut out the backing from the brocade. With right sides facing, pin the backing to the patchwork front. Stitch together, using a ½" (1.3 cm) seam allowance, leaving a 10" (25.4 cm) opening in one long edge for turning. Clip all curves, and turn right side out.

Tip: Add batting for a thicker rug, or jazz up a thinner rug with decorative quilt stitching over the patchwork layers before stitching everything together.

10. Using the patterns, cut two ears and one tail from the extra patchwork fabric cut from the patchwork front. Cut two ears and one tail from brocade. With right sides facing, pin each patchwork ear to each brocade ear. Pin a patchwork tail to a brocade tail. Stitch each using ¼" (6 mm) seam allowance, leaving a 2" (5.1 cm) opening in one long side for turning. Clip all curves, turn right side out, and press.

11. Stuff the ears and tail lightly with fiberfill and slipstitch the openings closed. With the brocade side facing down, hand sew the tail to the center back of the rug. With the brocade facing out, fold the base of each ear in half and tack the edges of the base together. Sew the ears to the rug, 4" (10.2 cm) from the sides of the rug and 9" (22.9 cm) from the tip. Have the brocade side of the ears facing the front of the rug.

12. Slipstitch the rug opening closed (See Slipstitch, see page 142.) Press.

Twig Dog Bed

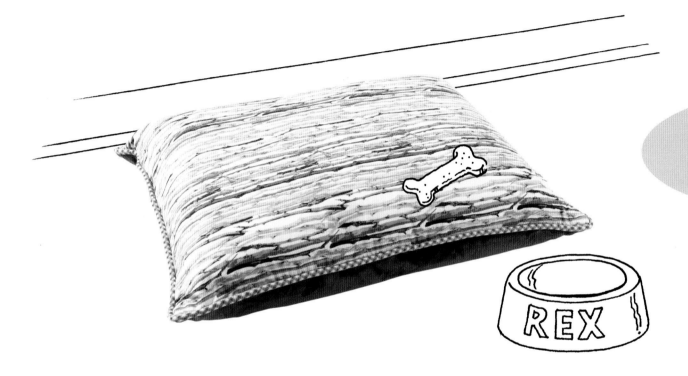

Fact: Did you know that there are 22 definitions of the word *fetch*? They include "to charm or captivate, to maneuver, and a trick."

Every dog is obsessed with playing fetch, so you can't go wrong with this one!

I'm sure many of you dog owners know what I mean, when I talk about my dog's unrelenting need to chase after and bring back sticks, balls, or just about anything. Duke would be in heaven if he could only take the day's sticks and twigs to bed with him. Now, with a twig-fabric dog bed, he can. (I can see it now, his paws twitching as he plays fetch in his sleep.) The right fabrics, custom-made into a floor pillow, will blend with your décor and are much more chic than a pet store bed. Standard pillow forms are 20" x 26" (50.8 x 66 cm) and 22" x 37" (55.9 x 94 cm)—perfect for most dogs.

Tip: To protect the pillow form, make a liner from Baby Dry Vinyl Fabric, a soft, water-resistant vinyl used for changing tables and baby bedding. Make it the same dimensions as the pillow form, but then make the outer cover slightly bigger.

Charm, the project designer's dog, is so fetching!

Tools:

❀ Hand sewing needle
❀ Pin
❀ Scissors
❀ Sewing machine
❀ Yardstick
❀ Zipper foot

Materials:

SMALL DOG BED
(for dogs 12 pounds [5.4 kg] and under)

❀ 1 yard (1 m) 45" (114.3 cm) -wide stick- or twig-inspired fabric
❀ 1 yard (1 m) 45" (114.3 cm) -wide cotton velour
❀ 3 yards (3 m) piping
❀ 20" x 26" (50.8 x 66 cm) machine-washable pillow form
❀ Matching thread

MEDIUM DOG BED
(for dogs up to 30 pounds [13.6 kg])

❀ 1¼ yard (1.25 m) 45" (114.3 cm) -wide stick- or twig-inspired fabric
❀ 1¼ yard (1.25 m) 45" (114.3 cm) -wide cotton velour
❀ 3½ yards (3.5 m) piping
❀ 22" x 37" (55.9 x 94 cm) machine-washable pillow form
❀ Matching thread

Instructions:

1. From each fabric, cut one 21" x 27" (53.3 x 68.6 cm) piece for the small dog bed, or one 23" x 38" (58.4 x 96.5 cm) piece for the medium dog bed. Cut a 95" (241.3 cm) length of piping for the small dog bed, or a 124" (315 cm) length for the medium dog bed.

2. Pin the piping to the right side of one fabric piece with the raw edge of the piping even with the fabric raw edge. Using the zipper foot, begin stitching in the center of the long back edge of the pillow top and 1½" (3.8 cm) from the beginning end of the piping. Stitch over the stitches that secure the cord inside the piping. Sew to 1" (2.5 cm) from the corner.

3. To turn the corner, keep the needle down and make three clips through the piping flange. Repeat for all corners. Continue stitching to within 1½" (3.8 cm) of the finishing end of the piping. Cut thread and remove from sewing machine.

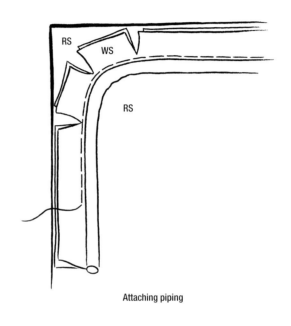

Step 3

RS

WS

RS

Attaching piping

4. To join the piping ends, remove several stitches that secure the cord inside the piping and open the fabric to expose the cord. Cut the cord so it is even with the beginning piping end.

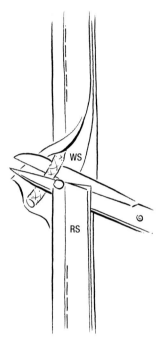

Step 4

WS

RS

Sewing piping in place

Step 5

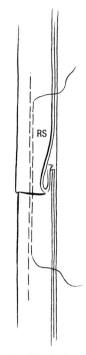

RS

Sewing piping in place

5. Fold the fabric ¼" (6 mm) to the wrong side on the finishing end and place the starting end of the piping on top of it. Pin the piping so the raw edge is even with the raw edge of the fabric. Using the zipper foot, sew it in place.

6. Place the pillow top and the bottom together, right sides facing and raw edges even. Using the zipper foot, sew the pieces together stitching over previous stitching and leaving an 18" (45.7 cm) opening in the center of the back edge for the small dog bed, or 25" (63.5 cm) for the medium dog bed.

7. Turn pillow cover right-side out. Insert the pillow form. Slipstitch the opening closed. (See Slipstitch, page 142)

Psychedelic Decoupage Plates

Fact: Jimi Hendrix was said to have associated colors with sounds. Purple was visualized as jealousy or anger, green as envy, and the colors of the rainbow as a special girl in his life.

You won't be eating off these plates, but you'll definitely be staring at them when you're done pasting psychedelic fabrics on your grandma's china.

Flashback to Jimi Hendrix's era with purple bell-bottom pants and outrageous album cover graphics. Even though I wasn't born in his era, I remember that when I was in college, dorm décor was definitely influenced by the '60s and '70s. It seemed that every student decorated his or her room with lava lamps and black light posters, rich with psychedelic colors. Decorating had to be cheap and it had to look cool.

We think this offbeat project, psychedelic decoupage plates, passes with flying colors! Combine heavily patterned plates, acquired from Grandma's mix-and-match cupboard, and busy, multipatterned fabrics that somehow work together (even if your initial thought is that they clash) for some really groovy and affordable wall art.

Tie-dye to die for

Instructions:

1. Decide whether you want the fabric on the rim or in the center of the plate. Use the pencil compass to draw the circles on the fabric. Cut out the circles.

2. Protect your workspace, and use the paintbrush to apply a thin coat of decoupage medium to both sides of the fabric. Be careful not to stretch the fabric.

3. Apply the fabric to the plate. Dampen the sponge and use it to press out air bubbles and smooth away wrinkles. Let dry.

4. Apply two more coats of decoupage medium, allowing each coat to dry thoroughly.

5. Secure the plate hangers on the plates and hang on the wall.

Tip: Découpage can be protected and given a ceramic-like sheen with three coats of high-gloss polyurethane. For best results, use #000 steel wool to lightly roughen the surface after the first and second coat.

Tools:

❀ Cellulose sponge
❀ Compass
❀ Paintbrush
❀ Scissors
❀ Water

Materials:

❀ Vintage plates
❀ Large scraps of print fabric
❀ Decoupage medium
❀ Plate hangers (measure plates to determine hanger sizes)

2

Giraffe Bolster Pillow

Tools:

❄ Hand sewing needle
❄ Iron and ironing board
❄ Lightweight cardboard
❄ Pins
❄ Sewing machine
❄ Scissors
❄ Press cloth
❄ Yardstick

Materials:

❄ 1 yard (0.9 m) 52" (132 cm) -wide medium-weight giraffe print fabric (See Resources on page 146: Fabric.com)
❄ ⅓ yard (0.3 m) medium-weight (any width) solid fabric
❄ 1½ yards (1.5 m) brown/black brush fringe trim
❄ Matching thread
❄ Contrasting thread
❄ 9" diameter x 48" long (22.9 x 121.9 cm) bolster pillow form
❄ Dritz® Fray Check (optional)

The long neck of the giraffe translates easily into an extra-long bolster pillow for creature comfort.

Animal prints have always been a designer's secret weapon, with a dash of zebra print here or a pinch of leopard there. While roaming through the zoo, we caught a glimpse of a goofy giraffe, with its striking graphic pattern. Not widely used, giraffe-print fabric has neutral coloration that blends easily into any home. We found the perfect project for it, so don't be afraid to stretch an exotic pattern at the head or foot of your bed.

Giraffes are one of nature's most remarkable works of art.

Fact: An adult giraffe eats up to 75 lbs (34 kg) of foliage a day. You'd think it wouldn't have time to be selective, but the giraffe only eats individual leaflets (from between sharp thorns) off the umbrella-shaped thorn trees of the African savannah.

Instructions:

1. Draw a 10" (25.4 cm) -diameter circle onto the cardboard. (See How to Draw a Circle, page 144.) Cut out for the bolster end pattern.

2. Cut a 30½" x 49" (77.5 x 124.5 cm) rectangle from the giraffe print for the bolster body. Using the bolster end pattern, cut two circles from the solid fabric. Cut a 48" (121.9 cm) length of fringe.

3. With right sides together, pin the fringe to one long edge of the bolster fabric, so the raw edge of the fabric aligns with the top of the fringe. This leaves ½" (1.3 cm) of fabric at each end without fringe. If the fringe ravels, apply Fray Check to the cut edges.

4. Sew the fringe ½" (1.3 cm) from the edge, backstitch at the beginning and end of the seam.

5. Fold the fabric in half with right sides together, fringe sandwiched between, and long edges even. Sew a ½" (1.3 cm) seam, leaving 16" (40.6 cm) open at the center. Press the seam open, using the press cloth.

6. Stay stitch ½" (1.3 cm) around the perimeter of each end of the bolster body piece. Staystitching is machine stitching through a single layer of fabric to reinforce the seamline so that you can clip into the seam allowance and spread it. Clip to the stay stitching every ½" (1.3 cm).

7. With the right sides facing, pin one open end of the bolster body to one bolster end, allowing the fabric to spread open where clipped. Sew a ½" (1.3 cm) seam, keeping the stay stitching just inside the seam allowance. Stitch directly over stitching for added strength. Repeat with other bolster end.

8. Turn the bolster right side out. Insert the bolster pillow form. Slipstitch the opening closed (See Slipstitch, page 142).

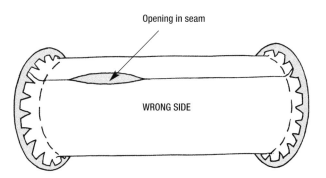

Opening in seam

WRONG SIDE

Marbleized Bookends

Wrap unused books with old-world charm to create an elegant set of bookends.

Tip: These bookends are a great place to hide precious documents, like that picture of your ex-boyfriend that you don't want your current boyfriend to see!

No trip to Italy is complete without stopping in a traditional *cartoleria*. These fine stationery stores sell beautiful, delicate paper goods. In Florence or Venice, you'll stumble upon a *cartoleria* as often as you might find a Starbucks in our cities and suburbs! Their windows display rich, marbleized leather journals, pencils, envelopes, bookplates, and desk accessories. You name it; it's marbleized. To bring the charm of old-world Italy into your home library, group a few hardback books together, adorn them with marbleized patterned fabric and leather, and *voilà*, a set of elegant bookends.

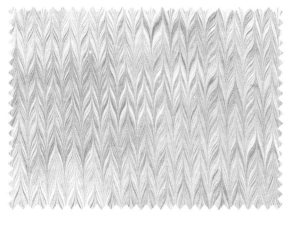

Marbleized paper evokes old-world charm.

Fact: The process of paper marbling is an ancient art of making paper look like marble. Color paints are sprinkled into a water bath. Patterns are created with combs or rakes that spread the colors into classic patterns, such as the fan-tail or marble vein pattern. Laying the paper on the surface of the water then transfers the pattern.

Instructions:

1. Remove the pages from a book by opening the front and back covers and using the craft knife to cut in the groove between the front cover and the pages. Reserve the book pages.

2. Open the covers flat and measure the width and the height. Add 2" (5.1 cm) to each dimension. Cut a rectangle of fabric that size. Mark the center of the rectangle's width and cut the fabric in half for the front and back cover.

3. Cut a strip of leather for the spine the width of the book spine plus ½" (1.3 cm) by the height of the cover plus 2" (5.1 cm).

4. Install leather machine needle into sewing machine and attach the walking foot. With right sides together and using a ¼" (6 mm) seam allowance, sew each side of the spine to the front and back fabric cover pieces. Finger press the seam allowance toward the spine.

5. Center the right side of the flattened book on the wrong side of the fabric assembly, aligning the book cover spine on the leather spine.

6. Apply the craft glue, with the Popsicle stick to spread a light, even coat to the inside of the covers. Fold each corner of the fabric at a 45 degree angle onto the book cover and glue. Be sure the fabric is slightly taut and is straight and smooth on the right side of the book cover. Then fold the straight edges of fabric onto the book cover and glue.

7. Glue the pages back into the book. Glue the first page to the inside of the front cover and the last page to the inside of the back cover. Close the book and place under a weight, such as a stack of books, and let dry.

8. Repeat steps 1 through 7 for each book. Arrange into two sets of three books each. Tie a leather or suede cord around the middle of each set.

Tools:

❀ Craft knife
❀ Popsicle stick
❀ Ruler
❀ Scissors
❀ Sewing machine
❀ Size 90/14 leather machine needle
❀ Walking presser foot
❀ White craft glue

Materials:

❀ Six old hardcover books in a variety of sizes (three books should be heavy enough to act as a bookend)
❀ Marbleized-print fabric
❀ Strips of garment-weight leather
❀ Matching thread
❀ Leather or suede cord

1

Cord Bin

Cover any small metal or plastic bin with earth-toned cording for an understated wastebasket, umbrella stand, or vessel for a home office, foyer, or bedroom.

Tip: If you're ambitious, or a spool of cording falls off the back of the truck, take a plastic industrial-size paint bucket, flip it over and create a cord-covered stool!

I remember making pottery in high school (art was my favorite class!). Our first project was to make coil clay pots, and if you showed the teacher that you could keep your pot from leaning, you might actually be allowed to touch the potter's wheel! But, back to coil clay pots. We began by rolling clay into "ropes" that we then coiled to form a cylinder. Thus, the inspiration for cord-covered bins!

Coiled boating line on the dock

Instructions:

1. Measure the circumference of the wastebasket at its widest point. Measure the height and divide by ¼" (6 mm) for the number of rows. Multiply the circumference by the number of rows. Divide by 36" (39.4 cm) for the amount of yards (meters) and round up to the next yard (meter).

2. Apply a band of hot glue around the bottom of the wastebasket. Adhere the cording, tucking the beginning end of the cording under the first row.

3. For each row, apply a band of hot glue and adhere the cording to the glue. Have each row abut the preceding row.

4. At the top, end on the same side as the starting point, tucking the finishing end of the cording under the row below.

Tip: Apply hot glue to the ends of the cording as soon as they are cut, to prevent them from untwisting.

Tools:

❀ Hot glue gun and glue sticks
❀ Scissors
❀ Tape measure

Materials:

❀ Small metal wastebasket or other metal or plastic container with smooth sides
❀ ¼" (6 mm) -diameter twisted rayon cording with no flange (See step 1 for estimating yardage.)

Royal Transfer Pillows

The crown jewels for your sofa!

These silhouetted pillows echo the shape of the transferred images. You can turn any printed image (magazine page, photo, clip art) into a pillow. Begin by finding appealing images with interesting shapes and cool graphics, such as these clip art gems. Use a transfer medium to reassign your image onto metallic silver and gold fabrics, for some serious bling. Cut and sew the silhouetted pillow. Then, embellish with glittery sequins and ostentatious beads. You might need to lock up these precious pillows so nobody steals them!

Tip: Imagine other graphic possibilities for these silhouetted pillows—animals, plants, muscle cars, or your boyfriend's or husband's picture, so you can hug him even when he's out of town!

Jewels are a girl's best friend.

Tools:

❀ Cellulose sponge
❀ Cardboard, slightly larger than image
❀ Crewel embroidery needle
❀ Hand sewing needle
❀ Iron and ironing board
❀ Paintbrush
❀ Paper towels
❀ Pencil
❀ Ruler
❀ Scissors
❀ Sewing machine
❀ Straight pins
❀ Tracing paper
❀ Tape
❀ Zipper foot

Materials:

❀ Plaid's Picture This Opaque transfer medium
❀ Dry-toner photocopies of desired images
❀ ½ yard (0.5 m) metallic fabric for each pillow front
❀ ½ yard (0.5 m) contrasting or solid color metallic fabric for each pillow back
❀ Beaded or sequined fringe, slightly longer than the length of the pillow perimeter
❀ Matching thread
❀ Polyester fiberfill
❀ Embellishments such as metal studs, rhinestone studs, pearls, large flat sequins, and metallic embroidery thread

Instructions:

1. Find images or clip art. Black and white antique engravings of two brooches and a crown were used here. Black-and-white or color will work with the transfer medium as long as the print is a dry-toner reproduction, such as a photocopy. The photocopy should be a flopped image, especially if it has wording, because the final transfer will be in reverse. Most copy shops can make oversized copies, so your pillow can exceed the boundaries of standard paper sizes. For best results, do not exceed the pillow sizes shown by more than a couple of inches (centimeters). Cut out the images, leaving a ¼" (6 mm) border all around.

2. To make the pattern for the pillow, place the image right side up and tape tracing paper over it. Trace the outline of the image onto the paper, and add 2" to 3" (5.1 to 7.6 cm) all around. (This includes a ½" (1.3 cm) seam allowance.) For best results, follow the general outline of the image so you have gentle curves and corners that are easy to sew, rather than sharp angles that might pucker the fabric. Cut out for the pattern. Set aside.

3. Cut a square piece of pillow front and pillow back fabric that is 6" (15.2 cm) larger all around than the image. Set pillow back fabric aside.

4. Work over a piece of cardboard. On the right side of the image, use the paintbrush to apply a thick, even coat of transfer medium to within ⅛" (3 mm) of the outer edge. Carefully place the image right side down on the right side of the pillow front fabric. Smooth it down with your fingers, then use the bottle of medium like a rolling pin, to spread the medium evenly, so the paper adheres to the fabric. The excess medium will ooze out beyond the edges of the paper. The oozed outline will create a raised edge that resembles an old wax seal. If needed, clean mess-ups immediately with a damp cloth. Lift the fabric off the cardboard to make sure they aren't sticking together. If they seem like they might stick, get a new piece of cardboard. Let the transfer cure and dry overnight.

5. To remove the paper from the transfer, place wet (damp, not soaking wet) paper towels on top for about ten minutes to soften the paper. With a wet cellulose sponge, rub the paper off to reveal the transferred image underneath. You won't get all the paper off in one shot, so stop and allow the transfer to dry, and then repeat the paper removal process. Consider leaving some bits of paper intact to give the image an antiqued look. When you have removed the paper, let the fabric dry completely.

6. Place the pillow front and back fabrics together so the wrong sides are facing. Place the pillow pattern on top of the transfer, making sure the image is centered in the pattern outline. Pin the pattern in place. Cut out both fabrics.

7. To attach the fringe, place the pillow front right side up on your work surface. Pin the fringe around the edge, starting in the center of the bottom edge, with the top edge of the fringe heading even with the raw edge of the fabric.

8. Using the zipper foot, begin stitching 1" (2.5 cm) from the beginning end of the fringe and ½" (1.3 cm) from the edge. At each corner (if your pillow has corners), insert the needle into the fabric and clip the heading up to the needle. Pivot the pillow front and continue sewing to within 2" (5.1 cm) of the end. Overlap the ends of the fringe, and finish sewing.

9. Refer to the photograph for suggested embellishment designs or create your own.

10. Once the pillow front is decorated, join pillow front and back with right sides together and fringe sandwiched between. Use a ½" (1.3 cm) seam and leave a 6" (15.2 cm) opening in one long edge. Clip the inner corners (if any) and clip evenly along the curved edges. Turn the pillow right side out. Press.

11. Stuff the pillow firmly with the fiberfill. Slipstitch the opening closed. (See Slipstitch, page 142.)

Water Lily Table Runner

Tip: Arrange lily pads on wash-away fabric stabilizer. After sewing the pads together (see instructions), carefully tear away the stabilizer.

Water lilies are the inspiration for this organic, asymmetrical table runner made with natural silks.

Riding a bike down the path along the Hudson River on the West Side of Manhattan, you'll discover pockets of nature. Sometimes, the only reminders we city folk have of nature's beauty are through idyllic, man-made sanctuaries or through our world-class museums. Monet's *Water Lilies* painting at the Museum of Modern Art always has an audience, and the little water lily pond in Battery Park, home to numerous koi and turtles, attracts the twelve-and-under set. Water lilies have always been engaging; how do they lie so flat across the surface of the water, how do some stick together and some wander away from the pack? If you prefer a more whimsical look, try using felt fabric. Felt doesn't require any edge finishing.

A pond of water lilies in a park on the West Side of Manhattan is peaceful and serene.

Tools:

❄ Craft knife and cutting mat
❄ Disappearing-ink fabric pen
❄ Iron and ironing board
❄ Lightweight cardboard 8" x 10" (20.3 x 25.4 cm)
❄ Pencil
❄ Pins
❄ Press cloth
❄ Sewing machine
❄ Small, sharp scissors

Materials:

❄ ½ yard (0.5 m) each 42" to 45" (106.7 to 114.3 cm) -wide dupioni silk in white, ecru, and beige
❄ ¼ yard (0.25 m) 42" to 45" (106.7 to 114.3 cm) -wide dupioni silk in light brown
❄ Thread in beige and light brown
❄ Dritz® Fray Check (optional)

Instructions:

FEEL FREE TO CHANGE THE COLORS AND ARRANGEMENT TO CREATE YOUR OWN ORGANIC TABLE TOP.

1. Enlarge the lily pad and flower patterns on a photocopier at 150%. Cut out patterns. (See Templates, page 156.)

2. Trace the lily pad and flower patterns onto the cardboard. Working on the cutting mat, cut out the patterns, using the craft knife.

3. To duplicate the example, trace the lily pad pattern twenty-four times each onto the white and ecru silks, and twenty times onto the beige silk. Trace the flower three times onto the light brown silk. Cut out.

4. Apply Fray Check to the edges of the silk cutouts, following the label directions, or allow the edges to fray, as shown. Another option is to finish the edges with an overlock stitch to prevent fraying.

5. Referring to the photograph, arrange and pin the lily pads in a rectangular shape that measures approximately 26" x 48" (66 x 121.9 cm). Make sure to distribute the colors evenly, layering most of the pads, and leaving the occasional small space open between them to create a delicate design. Also, make sure that most edges touch the edges of another lily pad, so when sewn, the lily pads become one piece.

6. With beige thread, topstitch ¼" (6 mm) from the edges of all the whole lily pads on the top layer. Next, topstitch only the visible edges of those lily pads on the next layer, then continue with the lily pads on the bottom layer. Press the piece from the wrong side, using the press cloth.

7. Arrange the lily flowers on the pads, as shown, then topstitch close to the edges using the light brown thread. Press from the wrong side, using the press cloth.

Belted Safari Shade

On a recent trip to Morocco, the designer's interest was piqued by campgrounds in the desert. Picture rough canvas tents with their fabric windows tied up. The natural colors and slouchy character of this window treatment mimic the desert scene, making it as fashionable as Yves Saint Laurent's signature safari pieces. It even has a pair of leather belts to hold it in its raised position, for a touch of haute couture. The shade is made with three ¼" (6 mm) dowels that help control the fabric. As ¼" (6 mm) dowels are only available up to 36" (91.4 cm) long, the shade is suitable for a window up to 38" (96.5 cm) wide.

An encampment in the desert

The safari, or traveling caravan, has long been a source of inspiration to many designers.

Tools:

❋ Awl
❋ Chenille needle, size 13
❋ Disappearing-ink fabric pen
❋ Iron and ironing board
❋ Pins
❋ Pliers
❋ Scissors
❋ Sewing machine
❋ Tape measure
❋ Yardstick

Materials:

❋ 54" (137.2 cm) -wide medium-weight fabric (see step 1 for determining yardage)
❋ ¼" x 1" (0.6 x 2.5 cm) lathe board, cut 1" (2.5 cm) shorter than window width
❋ Three ¼" (6 mm) -diameter wood dowels cut 1" (2.5 cm) shorter than window width
❋ Five or seven ½" (1.3 cm) -diameter screw eyes
❋ 2-ply nylon shade lift cord (three times the length of the shade plus the width)
❋ Two plastic cord drops
❋ Two large leather belts
❋ Two cup hooks
❋ Matching thread

Instructions:

1. Measure the width and height of the window. Add 2" (5.1 cm) to the width and 9" (22.9 cm) to the height. Purchase fabric based on these measurements, and cut out a rectangle.

2. Fold the side edges of the fabric ¼" (6 mm), then ¾" (1.9 cm) to the wrong side and pin. Sew close to the inside fold. Press.

3. For the lathe pocket at the top, fold the top edge ¼" (6 mm), then 3¾" to the wrong side and pin. Sew close to the inside fold. Press.

4. Fold the bottom edge ¼" (6 mm) then, 1¾" (4.4 cm) to the wrong side and pin. Sew close to the inside fold. Press.

5. To mark for the three dowel pockets, place the wrong side of the fabric face up. Measure from the stitching at the top to the bottom edge and divide that measurement by four. Beginning at the stitching at the top, use the fabric marker to mark the resulting measurement three times down both side edges.

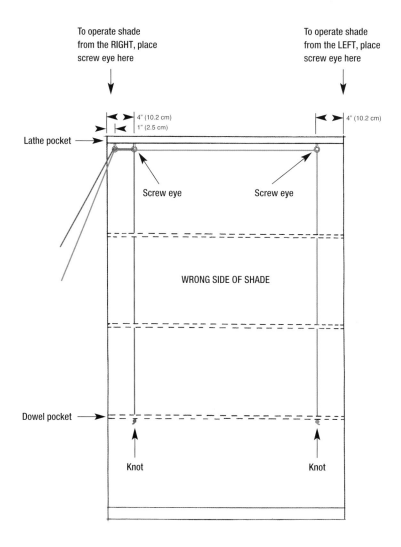

Threading the shade with cord

6. With the wrong side facing up, use the fabric marker and the yardstick to draw three lines across the rectangle, connecting the marks on the side edges.

7. With right sides together, fold along each line, pin, and press. Sew ½" (1.3 cm) from each fold to form the dowel pocket.

8. Insert the lathe into the pocket at the top, so the 1" (2.5 cm) sides are vertical in the pocket.

9. With the wrong side facing up, mark 4" (10.2 cm) in from both side edges of the lathe pocket. On the bottom ¼" (6 mm) side of the lathe, use the awl to make pilot holes through the fabric and into the lathe. Insert screw eyes into the holes and tighten with pliers.

10. Determine whether the shade will be raised and lowered at the right or at the left when it is hung. With the wrong side face up, secure another screw eye into the bottom ¼" (6 mm) side of the lathe, 1" (2.5 cm) from the chosen side edge. The illustration shows a shade that will be operated on the right when the shade is hung. To operate the shade from the left when it is hung, change the position of this screw eye to the other edge of the shade.

11. Insert a dowel into each dowel pocket.

12. With the wrong side facing up, mark 4" (10.2 cm) from both side edges on the fold of each dowel pocket.

13. Cut a length of cord one and one-half times the height of the shade. Thread it into the needle and make a knot in the end.

14. With the wrong siding face up and on the side of the shade that will be raised and lowered, insert the needle, at the mark, through the bottom dowel pocket. Have the knot against the dowel pocket. Sew through the other two dowel pockets at the marks. Insert the needle first through the screw eye 4" (10.2 cm) from the side edge, then through the screw eye 1" (2.5 cm) from the side edge. Refer to the red line on the illustration.

15. Cut a length of cord one and one-half times the height of the shade plus the width of the shade. Thread it into the needle and make a knot in the end.

16. Insert the needle through the remaining mark on the bottom dowel pocket. Have the knot against the dowel pocket. Sew through the other two dowel pockets at the marks. Insert the needle first through the screw eye immediately above, then through the two screw eyes on the other side edge of the shade. Refer to the green line on the illustration.

17. Trim the cords so they are equal lengths. Thread each end through a cord drop. Knot the end and conceal the knot inside the drop.

18. Locate the center of each belt. Center a belt at the top of the lattice pocket, 4" (10.2 cm) from a side edge. Position the buckle on the right side of the shade. Secure the belt to the top edge of the lathe using one or two screw eyes through the holes in the belt. (The number of screw eyes used depends on whether there are one or two rows of holes in the belt.) Secure the other belt centered 4" (10.2 cm) from the other outside edge.

19. Secure cup hooks into the underside of the top of the window frame, matching the location of the hooks with the screw eyes in the top of the lathe.

20. Hang the shade from the cup hooks. Pull on the cords to raise the shade, and then buckle the belts to secure the shade in its open position.

3

Corset Chair Cover

Designed to be shorter in length to expose more chair body, this slipcover shows some leg.

Fact: A "tightlacer" is someone who wears a corset for a minimum of fourteen hours per day. Ouch!

Inspired by the flirty elegance of camisole details and corset lacing, a basic dining chair was transformed by this sexy slipcover. It is corseted in the back to reveal the chair's spine and framework. Delicate satin straps attach the slipcover to the top of the chairlike camisole straps. Slip some on your dining set and get your damask on!

A black-leather corset has incredible sex appeal.

Tools:

* Disappearing-ink fabric pen
* Hand sewing needle
* Iron and ironing board
* Pins
* Ruler
* Sewing machine with overlock stitch
* Scissors
* Tape measure

Materials:

* Chair with square corners on the seat and back
* 1 yard (1 m) 54" (137.2 cm) -wide medium-weight fabric
* 3 yards (2.75 m) ¼" (6 mm) -wide double-face black satin ribbon
* 4 yards (3.75 m) ¼" (6 mm) -wide double-face ivory satin ribbon
* Matching thread

Instructions:

1. Refer to the schematic of measurements (right). For **A**, measure the width of the chair seat and add 13" (33 cm). For **B**, measure the seat depth from the front to the back. To that measurement, add the height of the chair back from the seat to the base of the top rail and add 8½" (21.6 cm). (2" [5.1 cm] at the top and 6½" [16.5] at the bottom.).

2. Cut a piece of fabric equal to the measurements, centering the pattern of the fabric, if applicable.

3. Draw the seat and back dimensions on the wrong side of the fabric, following the illustration. Draw the dashed line across the fabric as shown.

Schematic of Measurements

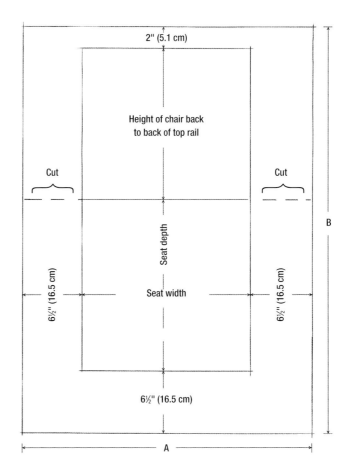

4. Referring to the illustration (on page 56), cut along the dashed line and overlock those raw edges.

5. Fold the remaining raw edges (not those that are overlocked) 6½" (16.5 cm) to the wrong side and press. With right sides facing, fold one front corner of the seat on a 45 degree angle, matching the pressed creases as shown. Sew along the vertical pressed crease. Trim the seam allowances to ¼" (6 mm). Press the seam open. Repeat for the other front corner. Turn right side out.

Step 5

Fold line

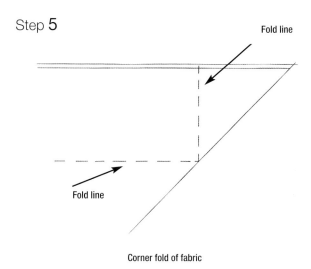

Fold line

Corner fold of fabric

6. Fold the lower edge of the chair seat ¼" (0.6 cm) to the wrong side, and ¼" (0.6 cm) again, and pin. Sew close to the outside fold, press.

7. Fold the side edges of the chair back 1" (2.5 cm) to the wrong side, and 1" (2.5 cm) again, and pin. Sew ⅞" (2.2 cm) from the outside fold, press.

8. Fold the top edge of the chair back 1" (1.3 cm) to the wrong side, and 1" (2.5 cm) again, and pin. Sew ⅞" (2.2 cm) from the outside fold, press.

9. Cut two 30" (76.2 cm) lengths of black ribbon for the lacing loops. With the wrong side of the chair back face up, and starting at the top of one side edge, fold the ribbon into 1" (2.5 cm) long loops, spaced approximately 1⅛" (2.8 cm) apart. Pin the bottom ¼" (6 mm) of each loop onto the fabric. Make approximately twelve loops, ending at the bottom of the side edge. To secure, sew ⅛" (0.3 cm) from the outside fold of the side edge. Repeat for the other side edge, making the same number of loops.

10. For the top ties, cut the rest of the ribbon into two 24" (61 cm) lengths. Fold each length in half and pin the fold to the wrong side of the top edge of the chair back, about 7" (17.8 cm) from the sides. Center the chair cover on the chair. Adjust the position of the top ties as needed, so they fall between vertical chair spindles. Remove the chair cover and hand sew the ties to the cover.

11. Place the cover on the chair. Tie the top ties to the top rail of the chair.

12. Thread the ivory ribbon through both top loops on the back of the chair cover. With the same amount of ribbon on each side, lace the ribbon through all the loops like lacing a shoe. Pull the laces tight and tie the ends into a bow.

Tip: If the ribbon you are using has the tendency to unravel, apply FrayCheck or clear nail polish to the ends.

Hanging Fabric File Folders

Bring energetic color to your home office using fabric remnants.

There is distinctive charm in the narrow, cobblestone streets of Venice, Italy, found in the form of the day's laundry. Textiles hang from open windows and delicate clotheslines. The randomness of color and texture offers a glimpse into the lives just inside the windows. Keeping this image in mind, create a cheerful collection of hanging fabric files that will brighten your office and distract you from the tedium of bill paying. Mix and match your own fabric scraps, or store-bought remnants, to give new life to boring files!

Hanging laundry in Italy proves that inspiration is everywhere.

Instructions:

1. Fold both long edges 1" (2.5 cm) to the wrong side twice. Press. Topstitch near the inner folded edge, then topstitch near the outer folded edge, on both sides. Press.

2. To form rod pockets on both short edges, fold the short edges ½" (1.3 cm) to wrong side. Press. Fold same edges 1" (2.5 cm) to wrong side. Press. Topstitch near the inner folded edges, and again along the top edge. Press.

3. Remove the metal rods from the paper file folder, and insert one through each of the rod pockets in the fabric file folder.

4. Repeat for as many fabric folders as you want. Hang fabric folders in filing container.

Tip: If you're afraid that you'll never find that bank statement, place marked paper tab-top file folders in your new fabric hanging file organizers.

Tools:

* Iron and ironing board
* Pins
* Scissors
* Sewing machine

Materials:

* Medium-weight cotton fabric, 16" x 22" (40.6 x 55.9 cm) (letter size), or 19" x 22" (48.3 x 55.9 cm) (legal size) for each folder
* Hanging file folder (paper), with metal hanging rods
* Matching thread

2

Antique Folding Room Screen

Tip: Depending on the height and width of the fabric panels, you can use this screen as a room divider, dressing room partition, or bed headboard.

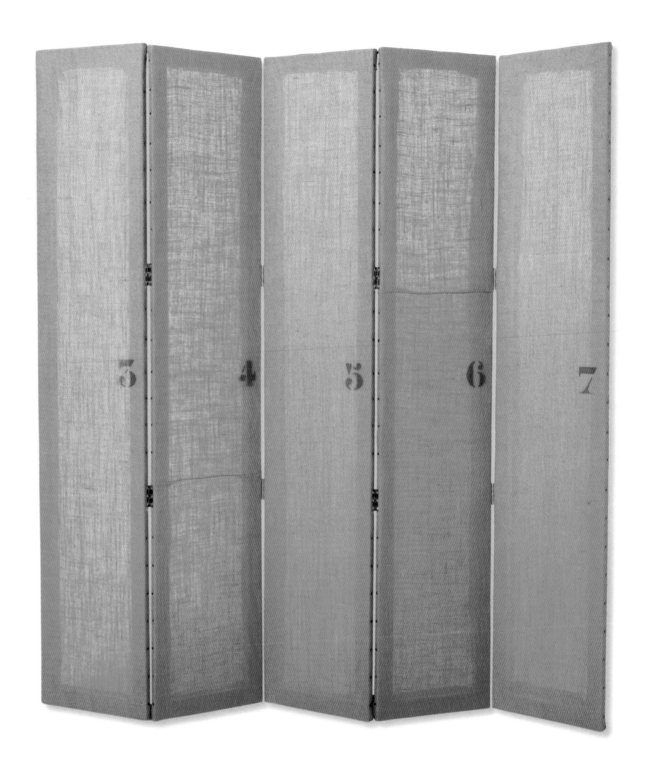

The compact design of this folding ruler with its aged color palette of burnt umber and worn espresso, inspired this folding room screen. We made the screen with burlap stretched between painter's stretchers, real nail heads, and imperfect graphic numbers, all influenced by the aesthetics of this outdated antique tool.

If you prefer decorative tacks to carpet tacks, make sure the tack heads don't extend more than ⅛" (3 mm), or the screen won't open completely. You will need 330 decorative head tacks for the top and sides of the panels and 30 carpet tacks for the bottom. Buy a stencil for the numbers or enlarge these on a photocopy machine, if you wish.

1 2 3
4 5 6
7 8 9
0

No longer suitable for measuring, this antique folding wooden ruler
is pleasing in its roughness and simplicity.

Tools:
❋ Awl
❋ Iron and ironing board
❋ Hammer
❋ Paper plate and paper towels
❋ Scissors
❋ Scrap paper
❋ Screwdriver
❋ Spray stencil adhesive
❋ Staple gun and staples
❋ Stencil brush
❋ Yardstick
❋ Copy machine (optional)

Materials:
❋ Ten 12" (30.5 cm) -long canvas stretcher strips
❋ Ten 60" (152.4 cm) -long canvas stretcher strips
❋ 4 yards (3.7 m) 56" (142.2 cm) -wide marigold-color burlap
❋ 2 oz. (59 ml) brown acrylic craft paint
❋ 2 oz. (59 ml) acrylic fabric medium
❋ Eight 2" (5.1 cm) -long hinges (with 3 screw holes in each plate)
❋ 60 wood screws
❋ Approximately 360 carpet tacks
❋ Premade number stencils, approximately 2¼" (5.7 cm) tall (optional)

Instructions:

1. Assemble the stretcher strips to make five panels.

2. Cut five 19" x 67" (48.3 x 170.1 cm) pieces of burlap. Press ½" (1.3 cm) to the wrong side on all raw edges.

3. Center a panel over the wrong side of a piece of burlap. Staple one long side of the burlap to the back of the panel. Staple to within 2" (5.1 cm) of the corners. Keeping the burlap taut, staple the long side opposite. Repeat for the two short sides. At each corner, fold the burlap in two inverted pleats, then staple the folds to secure. Repeat for the rest of the panels. (See How to Staple a Corner Fold, page 144)

4. Align a pair of panels with their right sides face down and long edges matching. Mark 20" (50.8 cm) from each end for the hinges. Secure one hinge at each mark. Use the awl to make pilot holes for the hinges before fastening with screws. Repeat with another pair of panels.

5. Turn the two pairs of panels with their right sides face up and matching the long edges. Align the remaining panel, with right side face up, on either side. Mark for the remaining hinges and secure the hinges.

6. Fold the screen closed. Hammer carpet tacks into the center edges of each panel 1" (2.5 cm) from the corners and 2" (5.1 cm) apart.

7. Open the screen. Working from left to right, randomly stencil numbers, (or refer to the photograph) onto the panels.

8. Following the manufacturer's directions, mix a dime-size amount of the acrylic color with the fabric medium on the paper plate.

9. Spray adhesive on the back of each stencil and position it on the screen.

10. Lightly dip the stencil brush into the paint mixture. (Very little paint is needed when stenciling.) Using a circular motion, brush the tip of the brush's bristles onto a pad of three or four paper towels. This removes excess paint and distributes the paint mixture evenly throughout the bristles. Using the same circular motion, lightly brush over the edge of the stencil, all around the number, and then into the center. Continue brushing until the paint coverage is even. Carefully lift stencil and continue to stencil other numbers. Allow the paint to dry three hours before moving the screen.

3

Blooming Dahlia Pillow

Doesn't the cylindrical base, made of garden-green, heavyweight fabric, resemble a flowerpot? From it sprouts a contrasting pink silk fabric in the form of a relief-like sculpture. The root of this pillow is hearty while the petals are delicate.

Fact: Dahlias were discovered by the Spanish in the mountains of Mexico, where they are the national flower. It is also the official flower of the city of Seattle, Washington.

This bright and beautiful accent pillow is perfect for that lazy chair in the corner of your preppy pink and green bedroom.

From a backyard dahlia in full bloom grows inspiration.

Tools:

* Compass
* Hand sewing needle
* Iron and ironing board
* Pins
* Ruler
* Tailor's chalk
* Sewing machine
* Zipper foot

Materials:

* 1 yard (.9 m) light-green, heavy- or upholstery-weight fabric
* Thread
* 1⅛ yard (1 m) 45" (114.3 cm) wide pink silklike fabric
* 2¼ yards (2.1 m) ⅜" (1 cm) cording
* 3" x 3" (7.6 x 7.6 cm) scrap of green felt or felted sweater (for flower center)
* Polyester fiberfill
* 5" x 7" (12.7 x 17.8 cm) piece of cardboard

Instructions:

1. Use the compass to draw a 6" (15.2 cm) -diameter circle on cardboard. Cut it out and use it to trace 42 circles onto the pink fabric. Cut out the circles.

2. Fold one of the circles in half with wrong side together. Use a loose, straight stitch to sew the curved edges of the circle together with wrong sides together. Do not knot or cut the thread.

3. Pull the thread gently to gather the piece, forming a petal. With the same thread, repeat step 2 with five more circles. Pull the thread tight and join it to the first petal to form a circle of six gathered and joined petals. Pull the thread tight and knot it several times.

Step 2

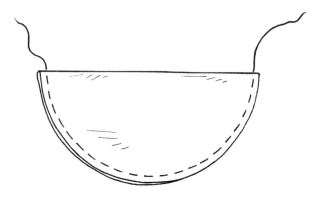

Step 3

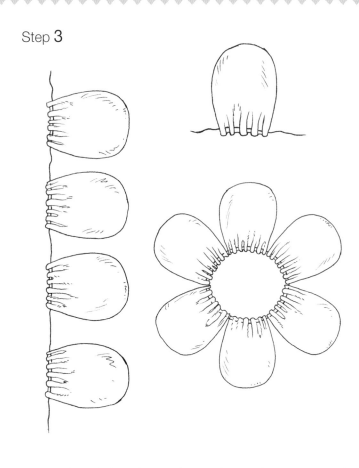

4. Make 3 more circles of 9, 12, and 15 petals respectively. The diameter of each circle gets slightly larger with more petals.

5. Cut two 12" (30.5 cm) -diameter circles from the green fabric (see How to Draw a Circle, page 144), a side piece 6" x 35" (15.2 x 88.9 cm), and two 2" x 38½" (5.1 x 97.8 cm) piping casement pieces.

6. Center and pin the ring of 15 petals on one of the green circles, about 3" (7.6 cm) from the outer edge. Hand sew the petals in place, stitching from the front to the back of the fabric, directly over the gathering stitches. Secure with a knot.

7. Sew the ring of 12 petals inside the ring of 15, and the ring of 9 inside the ring of 12, so that the pink circles look like a flower. Finally, sew the ring of 6 petals inside the ring of 9.

8. Cut a 3" (7.6 cm) -diameter circle from the scrap of green felt or felted sweater, and straight stitch (See Straight Stitch, page 142.) all the way around the edge of the circle. Pull the thread tight from both ends to gather the circle, making a little ball for the center of the flower. Stuff the flower center with a bit of polyester fiber fill. Tie the threads in a knot to secure.

9. Hand sew the flower center in the middle of petals.

10. All pillow seams are ½" (1.3 cm).

11. With right sides together, pin the short edges of the pillow side to form a circle. Stitch the seam, leaving a 4" (10.2 cm) opening in the center of the seam. This is where you turn and stuff the pillow.

12. With right sides together, sew the short ends of each piping casement piece together (to form a circle). Press seams open.

13. Cut the cording into two equal lengths. Lay one piece in the center of one of the casements (wrong side up). Trim the cording so it is the same length as the casement, hand stitch the cording ends together. Repeat with remaining cording and casement piece.

14. Fold the casement in half, around the cording. Use a zipper foot to sew the casement closed, close to the cording. Repeat for remaining casement and cording.

15. Pin the unfinished edge of the covered cording to the right side, outer edge of the petal-covered pillow top. Stitch, with the zipper foot. Repeat with remaining covered cording and pillow bottom.

16. Pin the right side of the pillow side piece it to the right side of the pillow top with the piping in between. Stitch with the zipper foot.

17. Repeat with the opposite side of the pillow side piece and the pillow bottom. Turn the pillow right side out through the opening in the pillow side.

18. Firmly stuff the pillow with fiberfill and hand sew the opening closed using a slipstitch. (see Slipstitch, page 142.)

1

Debonair Acrylic Tray

Serve James Bond a cold cocktail from a distinguished leather tray!

Tip: Try flipping the tray over and standing it on the handles to serve hors d'oeuvres! If you only intend to use it with the handles up, cover the screw heads with felt pads for a more detailed finish and to protect the table.

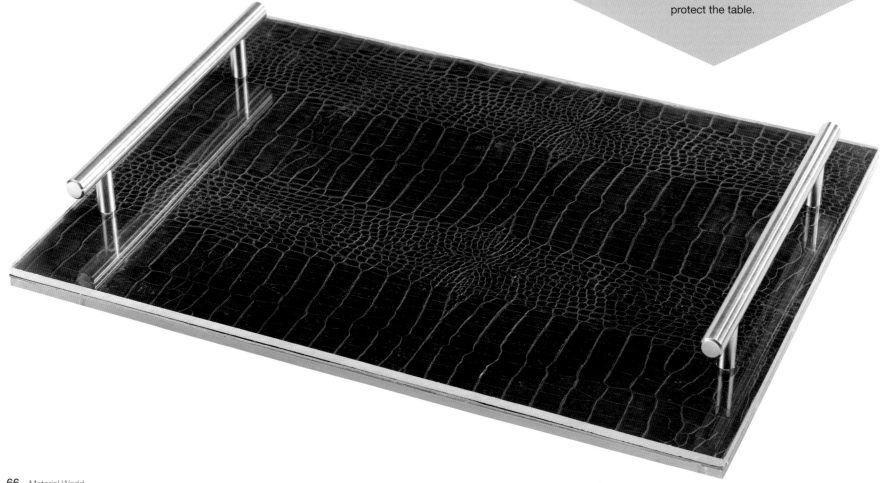

I am obsessed with collecting vintage barware and retro glassware. One of my sets has a decidedly masculine feel with retro black and gold graphics. Another set has metallic starbursts on thick clear glass, but my favorite cocktail stemware pieces are made of bronze glass. (I am definitely running out of NYC-apartment kitchen cabinet space.) Maybe I have been watching too many old James Bond movies, but I love entertaining with my collection.

Do you need something to serve your unique glassware on when you entertain? Make a custom serving tray that's as distinctive as your vintage glassware. Give it dual personas by sandwiching a scrap of crocodile-embossed leather (which comes in a variety of embossed patterns and has a clean edge when cut) and retro bark cloth (back to back) between two sheets of transparent plastic. You can flip the tray over and stand it on the handles to serve hors d'oeuvres! If you only intend to use it with the handles up, cover the screw heads with felt pads for a more detailed finish and to protect the table. Try shagreen, a roughened, granular, patterned leather for an über-expensive look; or for a disco glam feeling, use glitter vinyl and patent leather instead!

Always shaken, never stirred!

Instructions:

1. Lightly sand the edges of your precut pieces of acrylic.

2. Use a pencil to mark the wrong side of both materials with the dimensions of the precut acrylic, so the fabrics align perfectly with the edges of the acrylic.

3. Cut the fabric with scissors and the leather with the craft knife (on the cutting mat). Apply Stop Fraying fabric glue along the edges of the fabric.

4. With wrong sides together, sandwich the two material layers between the two pieces of acrylic. Hold the layers together temporarily with painter's masking tape. Center the handles on each of the short sides, 1" (2.5 cm) from the edge. Mark screw hole locations.

5. Drill holes to fit screws. Screw bolts from the bottom through the handles to the top.

6. Clean acrylic with window cleaner to get it party ready, and serve with style!

Tools:

❋ Craft knife and cutting mat
❋ Painter's masking tape
❋ Pencil
❋ Power drill
❋ Sandpaper
❋ Scissors

Materials:

❋ 2 sheets of ¼" (6 mm) acrylic (Lucite or Plexiglas), pre-cut to measure 12" x 14" (30.5 x 35.6 cm)
❋ One 13" x 15" (33 x 38.1 cm) piece of embossed leather
❋ One 13" x 15" (33 x 38.1 cm) piece of upholstery-weight fabric (bark cloth works well for a retro touch)
❋ Two cabinet pulls (sample shows 8¾" [22.2 cm] long, Euro-style handles; long length adds stability to the tray)
❋ Four long bolts (The screws that come with the handles may not be long enough.)
❋ Aleene's Stop Fraying Fabric Glue

Fact: Acrylic Plexiglas was developed in 1928 in various laboratories and was made public in 1933.

Kimono Table Runner

Create art for your table!

Fact: Traditionally, women's kimonos are one size, and are made from a single bolt of kimono fabric that is tucked and folded to fit the garment to the body. The level of formality is determined by the color and pattern of the fabric.

The intricate obi sash, worn with the Japanese kimono, inspired the rectilinear shape and fabric choices for this table runner. Opulent fabrics and complex folds, used to make an exotic kimono, are perfect for creating art for your table. Combine two boldly patterned fabrics and pleat them like origami for the top of the table runner, and use two complementary fabrics as backing. Display the finished piece on your dining table to accompany your next sushi dinner. Finished table runner is 17" x 59" (43.2 x 124.4 cm).

Japanese performers are visual masterpieces with their elaborate kimonos, obi belts, and precision dancing.

Tip: Pick up a book on origami. Paper cranes make excellent place card holders, in keeping with this table-topper.

Tools:

❀ Disappearing-ink fabric pen
❀ Iron and ironing board
❀ Pins
❀ Ruler
❀ Sewing machine
❀ Scissors

Materials:

❀ 1 yard (.9 m) kimono or Asian-inspired fabric
❀ 1 yard (.9 m) coordinating fabric for pleated panels
❀ 1 yard (.9 m) backing fabric for the center panel
❀ 1 yard (.9 m) backing fabric for the pleated panels
❀ Thread

Instructions:

1. Sew all seams with ½" (1.3 cm) seam allowance. Cut the following pieces of fabric:

> **CENTER PANEL:** (cut 1 of kimono fabric and cut 1 of backing fabric) 18" x 36" (45.7 x 91.4 cm)
>
> **PLEATED PANELS:** (cut 2 of decorative fabric for pleated ends and cut 2 of backing fabric for pleated ends) 34" x 13½" (86.4 x 34.3 cm)

2. Pin the right sides of the center panel pieces together and sew them together on both long ends. Turn the panel right side out and press the unfinished ends ½" (1.3 cm) to the wrong side.

3. Pin the right sides of one decorative and one backing pleated panel piece together. Stitch two short and one long side. Turn right side out and press. Repeat with remaining two pieces.

4. To mark pleated panel pieces, lay them with the unstitched ends on top, flat on your work surface, and use a ruler and fabric marking pen to draw fold lines every 3" (7.6 cm) from the right side.

Step 4

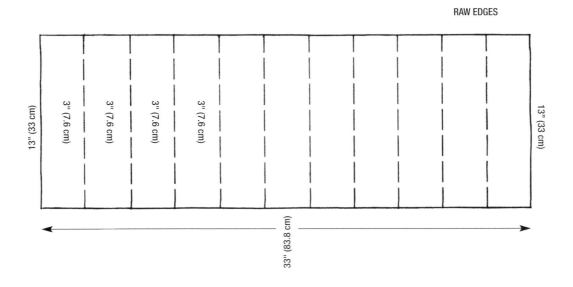

RAW EDGES

13" (33 cm)

3" (7.6 cm)   3" (7.6 cm)   3" (7.6 cm)   3" (7.6 cm)

13" (33 cm)

33" (83.8 cm)

5. Fold the fabric at the first marked line and bring it over to the second marked line. Pin it in place.

Step 5

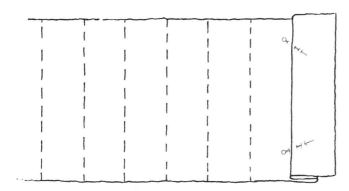

6. Continue folding and pinning the fabric to form five 3" (7.6 cm) pleats. Once all the pleats are folded the panel should measure 17" (43.2 cm). Baste across the top of the panel to hold the pleats in place.

Tip: If your pleated panel didn't come out exactly even, don't worry. Adjust or nudge the end pleats, so the pleated panel fits the center panel. It will still look fabulous!

7. Insert the unfinished end of the pleated panel ½" (1.3 cm) inside the open end of the center panel, pin. Topstitch across the folded edge of the center panel, catching the top edge of the pleated panel in the seam. Repeat at the opposite end with the remaining pleated panel. Press.

Recycled Denim Headboard Slipcover

Tip: Plan placement of the floral bloom appliqués with your bed pillows in mind. Make sure the pillows don't block the appliqués once your bed is made for the day.

W hen you daydream about kicking back and relaxing, you probably picture yourself in the country, wearing a pair of worn-out jeans as you lazily pick wildflowers. The reality might be a jam-packed closet in need of a denim edit, but do you have the heart to retire last season's blue jeans? Don't throw them away; recycle them into a slipcover for your headboard. Perhaps, if you stitch some floral appliqués on this denim headboard, your dreams will take you back to the country, with you and your alter ego picking daisies and whistling Dixie in your sleep. This is a queen-size headboard, made from a piece of ¾" (1.9 cm) plywood and a two by four (5.1 x 10.2 cm), cut to make two legs. It can rest behind the bed or be secured into the bed frame. If you want a more upholstered feeling, wrap the plywood with batting and make the slipcover a little bigger to accommodate it.

Can't part with your favorite blue jeans? Bring them to bed with you!

It's hard to beat the comfort of a favorite pair of jeans.

Tools:

❋ Fabric glue (optional)

❋ Iron and ironing board

❋ Disappearing-ink fabric pen

❋ Sewing machine (optional: with buttonhole or satin stitch capabilities)

❋ Sewing needle

❋ Scissors

Materials:

FOR A QUEEN-SIZE HEADBOARD SLIPCOVER, 60" x 32" x ¾" (152.4 x 81.3 x 1.9 cm):

❋ 3 pairs of old jeans

❋ 2 yards (1.8 m) fabric for the back of the slipcover (lightweight denim works well)

❋ Craft paper

❋ Scraps of flower-printed fabrics

❋ Handful of fiberfill

❋ Thread

Instructions:

1. Cut the seams out of the legs of old jeans so you are left with strips of denim that can be sewn together to form the slipcover. Trim the sides so they are relatively straight.

2. Align the bottom hems of the jeans to make the finished bottom edge of the cover. With right sides together, sew the jeans legs together, starting at the hems. Press the seams open and zigzag or overlock the raw edges. Repeat until all the jean pieces are joined.

3. Measure the height and width of the headboard you intend to cover. To accommodate the depth of the headboard, you need to make a boxing strip that joins the front and back pieces. Cut the fabric as below.

4. With right sides together, sew the short sides of the three boxing strips together, with the longer strip in the middle. Pres the seams open. Stitch around the corners to strengthen them, ⅜" (1 cm) from the edge.

FABRIC MEASUREMENTS FOR BOXING STRIP:

WIDTH for all Pieces = the thickness of the headboard + 1" (2.5 cm) for seam allowances

LENGTH for 2 Boxing Strip Side Pieces: headboard height + 1" (2.5 cm) for hem + ½" (1.3 cm) for seam allowance

LENGTH for 1 Boxing Strip Top Piece: headboard width + 1" (2.5 cm) for seam allowances

CUTTING FABRIC MEASUREMENTS:

Headboard Back (Fabric)

Add 1" (2.5 cm) to the width of the headboard for seam allowances.

Add ½" (1.3 cm) to the height of the headboard for the seam allowance and 1" (2.5 cm) for the hem.

Headboard Front (Pieced jeans)

Add 1" (2.5 cm) to the width width of the headboard for seam allowances.

Add ½" (1.3 cm) to the height of the headboard for the top seam allowance. (The bottom is already hemmed.)

5. With right sides together, pin the boxing strip to the slipcover back with raw edges even. Clip the seam allowance of the boxing strip at the seam (where it meets the slipcover corner).

Step 6

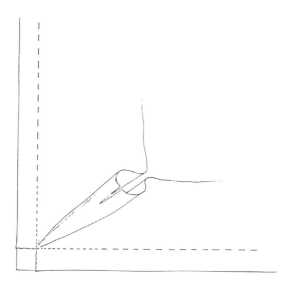

FOR THE APPLIQUÉS:

MAKE FLORAL APPLIQUÉS TO BLOSSOM ON THE SLIPCOVER. USE FABRICS WITH LARGE FLORAL PRINTS THAT CAN BE CUT OUT AND CREATIVELY COMBINED.

1. Cut out flower motifs from a variety of fabrics. Layer each motif onto a scrap of denim or other fabric. Denim works great because the edges can be frayed for added texture. By machine, zigzag or satin stitch the flower motif to the backing around the perimeter of the blossom. Use matching or contrast thread.

2. For added dimension, partially stitch one motif and then fill it with the fiberfill. Continue stitching until the entire perimeter is finished.

3. Arrange the appliqués on the headboard and stitch or glue them in place. Don't be afraid to overlap and/or leave some edges unattached so it looks like a flower garden.

6. Stitch ½" (1.3 cm) seam, shortening the stitch length near the corners. Stitch slowly near the corner and take one or two diagonal stitches across the corner, folding the boxing strip fabric out of the way. Repeat at other corner and finish the seam. Press seam open and zigzag or overlock seam allowances (if the fabric ravels).

7. Hem the bottom of the boxing strip and slipcover back, by pressing ½" (1.3 cm) to the wrong side, and then ½" (1.3 cm) again. Stitch close to the inside folded edge.

8. With right sides together, pin the front of the slipcover to the remaining side of the boxing strip with lower edges matching. Refer to steps 5 and 6 for instructions. Press.

Tip: It takes roughly 3 pairs of jeans to make 9 single panels for a queen-size slipcover. If you have a short inseam and a large headboard, you might need more jeans. If necessary, to accomodate the height of the headboard, patch two legs together per panel, or make a shorter plywood headboard.

Fancy Plants Chair

Tip: Make a quirky set of dining chairs with Philippe Starck vision! First, find enough chairs for your dining table. Don't worry about finding a matching set. You can make them match by painting all the wood chair frames glossy black (or your favorite color) and reupholstering the seats and back with the same fabric. Switch up the graphic on each seat back to keep each chair one of a kind!

Armed with some fabric, you can transform a lowly chair into a seat fit for a king. The project designer picked up this particular chair for five bucks. (Wow, it cost me a lot more to ship it to the photo studio). It was transformed it into a fancy chair, perfect for the corner of a bedroom or plush desk seating. White canvas, appliquéd with a graphic, black plant motif looks clean and refreshing, while painting the chair frame black added a sharp, modern edge. Try to find a chair with cushions that are in fairly good shape and that has the upholstery mounted to the frame, not around the cushions.

Ugly, upholstered dining room chairs, found at a yard sale or flea market are worthy of a second look! Really!

Black and white plant life, silhouetted against the dusty sky, is elegant in its simplicity.

Tools:

❁ Pliers
❁ Construction solvent (for chair prep)
❁ Plastic bag
❁ Fine sandpaper for between coats of paint
❁ Paintbrush
❁ Iron and ironing board
❁ Press cloth
❁ Paper-backed fusible web
❁ Staple gun and staples
❁ Fabric glue
❁ Sewing machine (with buttonhole stitch capabilities)

Materials:

❁ Upholstered dining room chair
❁ White heavyweight fabric (yardage determined by the existing amount of upholstery)
❁ Remnant of black cotton fabric, enough to cut appliqué motif
❁ Thread
❁ Black high-gloss paint
❁ Black gimp trim (enough to fit around the perimeter of the upholstery)

Instructions:

1. Strip the chair by removing all trim, fabric, and staples. Take notes as you remove layers, so you remember how to put it all back together. Use pliers to pull out staples, and construction solvent to dissolve any adhesives. Keep the fabric intact so you can use it as the pattern for the new fabric pieces.

Tip: Once you remove the fabric, if you find the foam in bad shape, go to a craft or sewing supply store and have new pieces cut to match the dimensions and shape of the existing foam.

2. Sand, paint, and refinish the chair frame with 3 to 4 coats of high-gloss paint.

3. Press the fabric you removed from the chair and use it as the pattern to cut out the same exact pieces from your new fabric. To be safe, add an extra 1" (2.5 cm) of fabric all around; it can always be trimmed away later. Cut the same exact pieces as the original chair. The chair shown here had two pieces for the seat and two for the back; one cut to size and another with hem allowance to fold and wrap over the foam.

4. Enlarge the plant motif on a photocopier machine 300%, or draw a freeform stem with organic shaped leaves and trace them onto the black fabric. (See Templates, page 160.)

5. Follow manufacturer's instructions to fuse the paper-backed web onto the wrong side of the black fabric. Cut out the motif and hold it up to the chair to determine the best position. It might work best on the seat back or it might look great growing on the seat.

6. Remove the paper backing and fuse the appliqué onto the fabric at the desired location. Machine stitch with a zigzag, buttonhole, or appliqué stitch around all the edges of the motif. Feel free to add details, like stems and stamen, with additional embroidery.

7. Put all the pieces of the chair back together the same way the pieces came off. Every chair is different, so refer to your notes from step one. The illustration shows the pieces that came off and then went back on this chair.

8. To staple the new upholstery, follow a 'north/south/east/west' pattern to keep the fabric smooth. Position the fabric on the foam and wrap it around the foam, board backing and fabric back piece. Pull and staple the center of each side taut and even (but not stretched)(north side first, then south, followed by east and then west). Then, pull and staple the corners. Fill in the remaining sides with staples.

9. Place the newly covered cushion back in the frame. Cover the staples and finish all the edges by gluing gimp along the chair back and seat covers.

FRONT PIECE OF FABRIC
(With extra seam allowance)

FOAM

BOARD BACKING
(exact size of inside
back frame)

FABRIC BACK PIECE
(Cut exactly to size of board)
Right side down

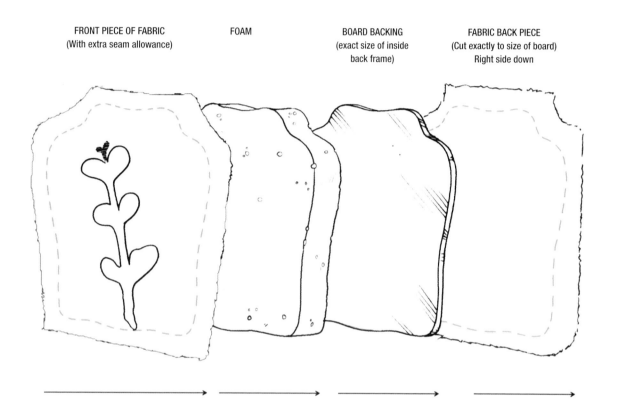

BACK OF CHAIR

Oxford Shirt Cushion Cover

Retire one of your boyfriend's (or husband's) old oxford button-front shirts (preferably one he no longer wears) and transform it into a feminine pillow for your couch. Boy, will he be surprised and you'll feel good recycling an old shirt into something new for the home! Save yourself sewing time by using the button placket from the shirt as the closure for the cushion cover.

Fact: Oxford is a type of weave used to make the fabric in oxford cloth shirts. The warp has two fine yarns paired together, and the weft has heavier fill yarn, which gives the fabric a subtle basket-weave appearance.

Enjoy the classic comfort of a man's oxford shirt.

Tools:

❋ Iron and ironing board
❋ Ruler
❋ Sewing machine
❋ Scissors
❋ Tracing paper and pencil

Materials:

❋ One small- or medium-size pillow insert
❋ One XL cotton, long-sleeved men's shirt with front button closing
❋ Thread

Instructions:

1. Cut the shirt open at side seams, shoulder seams, and sleeve seams. Cut off collar. Press pieces flat.

2. Measure the length and width of the cushion, add 1" (2.5 cm) to both measurements, and draw a paper pattern to match the measurements.

3. Close the buttons on the front of the shirt piece and center the pattern over the buttons. Cut the pillow back from the front of the shirt.

4. Cut the pillow front from the back of the shirt.

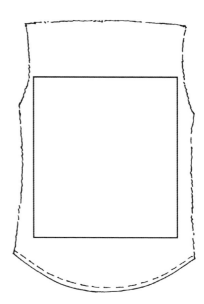

Step 4

Step 3

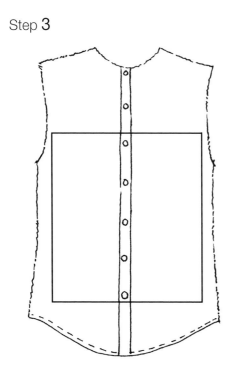

5. Use the remaining shirt pieces to make the ruffles. The more ruffles, the better, so don't waste any fabric. Draw various sized spiral shapes with pencil all over remaining pieces of shirt and cut them out.

Step 5

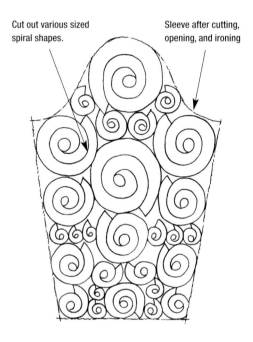

Cut out various sized spiral shapes.

Sleeve after cutting, opening, and ironing

6. Uncurl the spiral shapes so that they are straight. This will create the ruffle effect. Pin the edges of the ruffle strips to the pillow front, and stitch along any lengthwise edge in a random pattern. Leave ½" (1.3 cm) clear around the pillow front and back edges for seaming the pieces together. Layer each strip, and continue until the entire front cushion panel is covered.

Step 6

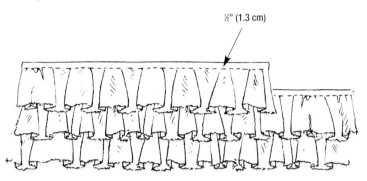

½" (1.3 cm)

7. Pin pillow front and back with right sides together around all sides. Stitch with ½" (1.3 cm) seam allowance. Stitch over the placket area a second time to reinforce it.

8. Open the buttons to turn the cover right side out.

9. To fray the ruffle edges, machine wash and dry the pillow cover.

10. Insert the cushion in the cover, and wait for your boyfriend's reaction! (Warning: the boyfriend species usually doesn't notice environmental changes unless he's an architect or interior designer.)

Heartfelt Toaster Cozy

Tools:

❁ Hot glue and glue sticks
❁ Pins
❁ Ruler
❁ Scissors
❁ Sewing machine

Materials:

❁ ½ yard (.5 m) yellow felt
❁ 1 yard (.9 m) ball fringe
❁ Pencil
❁ Scraps of felt in various colors: purple, orange, gray, pink, brown, gold
❁ Scrap of polyester fiberfill
❁ Thread

Tip: As a safety precaution, unplug your toaster when it's wearing its colorful cozy.

More often then not, the toaster is just another unsightly appliance, taking up space on your kitchen countertop. A toaster cozy takes care of that and brightens up your day. Directions are for a 12" x 10" x 6" (30.5 x 25.5 x 15.2 cm) toaster. Customize your cozy with graphic motifs reminiscent of your childhood sticker album.

It's pretty cool when an appliance can double as art!

Give back to the toaster that toasts your toast!

Instructions:

1. Cut 3 pieces of yellow felt 9" x 12" (22.9 x 30.5 cm) for the front (2) and back (1) of the toaster cozy. Reshape the two top corners of one of the pieces (by tracing around a small plate) so the corners are more curved than square. Use it to trace the same shape on the two remaining pieces.

2. Cut one piece 6" x 30" (15.2 x 76.2 cm) for between the front and back pieces.

3. Cut arched pieces for the rainbow and hearts from felt scraps, or cut other motifs of your choosing. (See Templates, page 157.)

4. Position motifs on one yellow piece. Once you are satisfied with the placement, glue or stitch them in place.

5. Place a second yellow piece under the decorated piece and baste around the edges with ¼" (6 mm) seam. Leave a 6" (15.2 cm) opening on the bottom.

6. With right sides together, pin the long strip to the decorated front, starting the bottom, up one side, across the top and down the remaining side. Clip into the seam allowance at the corners to help ease around the corners. Sew the pieces together with ½" (1.3 cm) seam.

7. Pin the remaining felt piece to the opposite side of the strip with right sides together and repeat step 6.

8. Lightly stuff the fiberfill into the front of the cozy through the opening. Sew the opening closed.

9. Pin ball fringe to the bottom of the cozy. Fold ends to wrong side for neater finish.

10. Machine stitch on top of the trim heading to secure it to the toaster cozy.

11. Place your heartfelt cozy over your toaster and admire!

Step 1

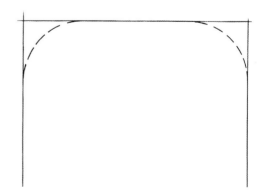

Interfaced Room Partition

Fact: Is it a coincidence that three different designers chose grommets as their preferred method of hanging hardware for their projects? There is no pinch pleating going on in this book! Grommets are a modern application, a simple method many designers use. Whether they appear on an S-curve curtain, flat-panel room partition, corset top, or an understated shower curtain, different-size grommets are everywhere.

Room partitions or dividers are an attractive and functional solution for masking your bedroom futon from your makeshift living room/entertaining area. A peanut butter and jelly sandwich serves up the inspiration for this interfaced partition project. Layer decorative fabrics and "glue" them together with fusible interfacing that acts like the sticky peanut butter, when activated by heat from an iron. Extra jelly like goodies are sandwiched within the fabric panels and ooze out of apertures. Hang your finished partition from the ceiling with single screw hooks spaced to match grommet locations, or from a curtain rod attached to the ceiling for a retractable panel.

Layers of peanut butter and jelly make a sandwich that looks as good as it tastes.

Do you have a studio apartment that you live and work in? Create a groovy fabric partition without a sewing machine!

Tools:

❋ Disappearing-ink fabric pen
❋ Fabric spray adhesive
❋ Iron and ironing board
❋ Paper
❋ Pencil
❋ Pins
❋ Press cloth

Materials:

❋ 4 yards (3.7 m) of 45" (114.3cm) -wide, medium-weight black fusible cotton broadcloth
❋ 2 yards (1.8 m) cool patterned cotton or cotton/blend fabric
❋ 1 yard (.9 m) medium-weight white fabric
❋ Six ⅝" (1.6 cm) grommets and grommet kit
❋ Ball chain links, rope, or ribbon to hang the partition

Instructions:

PARTITION IS 44" (111.8 CM) WIDE × 72" (1.8 M) LONG

1. Cut two panels, each the width of the fabric and 2 yards (1.8 m) long of the solid black fusible fabric. Adjust the dimensions of the panel to fit your room.

2. Fold and finger press 1" (2.5 cm) around all four edges to the inside of each panel.

3. Lay the panels on the floor with the fusible sides facing each other. Pin around all four sides and across the center of the panel so all edges align.

4. Use the fabric pen to sketch a graphic and random design onto the top panel. The example shows teardrop paisley shapes, but you can draw any shape.

5. Cut the shapes out with scissors to create openings for the patterned/white fabric to peek through. Trace the outline of the shapes onto paper and add 2" (5.1 cm) all around.

6. Fold the patterned fabric in half and keep the white fabric a single layer, and trace these shapes onto the patterned and/or white fabric. Cut out as many shapes as planned in step 4.

7. Lightly spray the wrong side of one of the patterned cut-out shapes with fabric adhesive. Place the corresponding piece over it so wrong sides are together. Smooth it and let dry. Repeat for all patterned shapes.

8. Insert the double-layer patterned shapes and single layer white shapes between the black interfacing layers so they are visible through the cut-outs and visually appealing (from both sides). Pin the shapes in place.

9. Set the iron to the temperature recommended for the fabric. Iron the entire panel, (use a press cloth to protect the iron) removing pins as you go. Work from one corner slowly to the opposite corner to fuse both black panels, locking both the patterned and white fabrics within.

10. Cut openings within the white fabric pieces to create windows.

11. Measure and mark grommet locations evenly across the top of the panel (about 8" (20.4 cm) apart). Attach grommets, following the instructions on the grommet kit.

12. Create loops for hanging the partition with ball chain links, rope, or ribbon.

1

Lace Table

This flashback to the '80s inspired the fuchsia lace embellishment, giving this modern table a retro look.

Tools:

❀ Foam brush
❀ Scissors

Materials:

❀ 9 yards (8.2 m) fuchsia lace ribbon with two scalloped edges (try to match the ribbon width with the table leg width)
❀ White table (18" x 18" x 18" [45.7 x 45.7 x 45.7 cm])
❀ White glue
❀ Water
❀ Clear acrylic topcoat sealer, gloss finish

The 1980s had fashion ups and downs, with DayGlo socks, rubber bracelets, acid washed and zippered jeans, inspired by pop royalty like Michael Jackson and Madonna. For girls, the colors were bold, hair was big, and the fabric of choice was lace. Lace, once a fabric of innocence, became a symbol of rebellion when worn by "the material girl." In the movie *Sixteen Candles*, an American coming-of-age film, Molly Ringwald inspired girls everywhere to customize their own outfits and dye satin shoes to match their prom dresses. I went to my first prom in a ruffled, mauve lace and satin number!

Prom shoes from the 1980s have a story to tell; if only they could talk!

Instructions:

1. Use the table as a guide to measure the lace embellishment to go around the perimeter of the top, around the sides of the table, and down the outer sides of each leg.

2. Starting at one corner of the tabletop, position the lace ribbon ⅛" (3 mm) from the table edge; when you get to each corner, cut lace at a mitered angle for a clean detail. Set the four cut pieces aside.

3. Starting at a corner, wrap a continuous piece of lace around the sides of the table (as shown) to determine the correct length. Cut the piece and set it aside. If necessary, trim the width of the lace to fit the table edge.

4. Measure the length of the table legs and cut two pieces of lace for each leg. Again, trim the width of the lace, as needed so it fits the legs.

5. Mix a simple decoupage adhesive of white glue and water. Combine and stir ingredients until you have a thin paste that goes on smooth.

6. Dip a piece of lace into the mixture and use your index and middle fingers to smooth the adhesive paste onto the lace.

7. Place the lace on table and smooth it down.

8. Continue steps 6 and 7 for each piece of lace. Wait for the glue to dry

9. Apply four coats of clear topcoat sealer to the entire table, including legs, with a foam brush. Let the sealer dry between coats, per the manufacturer's instructions.

Step 2

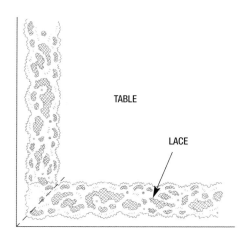

TABLE

LACE

Fern and Fish Shower Curtain

Inspired by elements from the sea and in the woods, there's something fishy about this shower curtain.

Tip: Painter's canvas can be purchased wide enough for a shower curtain, which is typically 72" (182.8 cm) wide. If you choose to use a different fabric, you might need to piece it to obtain the necessary width.

Ferns and leaves make excellent materials for imprinting; so do fish (yes, real fish). The designer of this project printed several types of fish and a variety of organic shapes in vibrant colors on natural-colored painter's canvas, to give this shower curtain a lot of personality. With the fish swimming in all directions, a feeling of movement comes alive on the canvas. Cruise through your backyard, and then hit your local fish market for inspiration and for materials to imprint on your own shower curtain. Try to complete this project in one day, because the fish can get a little smelly after that!

The ocean floor is a peaceful environment.

Tools:

❋ Grommet kit
❋ Iron and ironing board
❋ Paintbrush
❋ Sewing machine

Materials:

❋ 2⅛ yards (1.9 m) 72" (1.8 m) -wide painter's canvas
❋ Matching thread
❋ Twelve 1" (2.5 cm) grommets
❋ Shower curtain hooks
❋ Fabric paint in assorted colors
❋ 12" x 16" (30.5 x 40.6 cm) piece of plywood
❋ Several sheets of blank paper
❋ Real fish from your local fishmonger, such as red snapper, flounder, porgy, butterfish, and white fish
❋ Leaves of your choice, such as fern leaves
❋ 1 lemon
❋ Assorted glass beads
❋ Embellishing glue

Instructions:

1. Hem the sides of the canvas, by turning under ½" (1.3 cm) and then ½" (1.3 cm) again and stitching along the inside fold. Press.

2. Hem the bottom and top of the canvas by turning under ¼" (6 mm) and then 2" (5.1 cm) and stitching along the inside fold. Press.

3. Attach 12 evenly spaced grommets to the top of the curtain, following the instructions on the grommet kit.

4. Place the shower curtain on a large table and plan the colors and placement of your fish and fauna. To keep the project easy, make each fish its own color, so you don't have to keep washing and drying the fish. It might help to sketch the plan on paper first. Start with the leaves to create the environment for your fish to swim in. Apply a lot of paint to the first branch or leaf. Place the painted flora on the canvas and cover it with plain paper and then the piece of plywood. Press down hard on the plywood. Let it sit for a minute, remove the plywood and paper, and then gently peel off the leaf. Repeat with other branches and/or different leaves.

5. Wash and dry your fish. Be careful not to squeeze them or their insides might ooze out!

6. Start with the largest fish and apply paint to one side. Position the fish on the canvas (as planned), gently unfurling the fins and tail, while holding it in place. Gently press the head and tail into the canvas with a small rocking movement. Remove the fish with one quick swoop.

7. Refer to your plan and add more paint to the fish. Print it as many times as desired.

8. Switch to a new fish and paint color, and keep going until you are delighted with the shower curtain.

9. Let the curtain dry.

10. Cut a lemon and squeeze it onto your hands to get rid of the stinky fish smell.

11. After the paint has dried, add life to your fish by gluing on glass beads for eyes and for air bubbles. Let the glue dry overnight. Hang the shower curtain with the shower hooks.

2

Rich Bohemian Table Cover

Bring the Marrakech Express to your living room with a richly ornate table cover.

Fact: The Gwalior Fort is one of the oldest forts in Madhya Pradesh, India. It was built in the 15th century and spreads out over an area of 3 square km, (1.2 square miles) bound by solid walls of sandstone. It encloses 3 temples and 6 palaces.

Tools:

* Disappearing-ink fabric pen
* Iron and ironing board
* Ruler
* Sewing machine
* Scissors

Materials:

* 28" (71.1 cm) square piece for top fabric
* 1½ yards (1.4 m) bottom fabric
* 2 yards (1.8 m) natural fringe
* Thread

The façade of Gwalior Fort in Madhya Pradesh, India

The architectural depth, intricate stonework, and rich color of the facade of Gwalior Fort in India is reincarnated as a bohemian fashion and home design influence around the world. The boldly ornate bohemian style is inspired by the art and culture of India. It combines rich textures through layering heavily patterned fabrics.

This plain side table is covered with two luxe fabrics that parallel the ornamental design of Gwalior Fort. Taking a cue from the building's blue color and intricate design, the fabrics mimic the facade. The fringe represents the visual break where the two stone textures meet.

Instructions:

INSTRUCTIONS TO FIT 16" (40.6 CM) SQUARE TABLE:

FOR THE TABLE TOPPER:

1. Turn the top fabric to wrong side and draw cutting lines 6" (15.2 cm) from each side with the fabric marking pen.

2. Cut away the four corners created by the marked lines. See illustration at right.

3. Zigzag stitch around all the raw edges, pivoting at the corners to keep the fabric from fraying. Use a wide, dense zigzag stitch.

4. Pin the fringe to the right side, along the bottom of each outside edge. Fold the ends to the wrong side and topstitch the fringe in place. If the fringe heading is wide, stitch a second row of topstitching to better secure the fringe.

FOR THE BOTTOM TABLE LAYER:

1. Cut 5 pieces of fabric, each 17" (43.2 cm) square. Set one square aside. Hem three sides of the other four squares by pressing ¼" (6 mm) to the wrong side, and then ¼" (6 mm) again. Stitch close to the inside fold.

2. With right sides together, stitch the unfinished edge of each square to one side of the remaining square. (This creates the shape of a plus sign). Press the seams open and zigzag or overlock all the raw edges.

3. Layer the two fabrics on the table for a rich, bohemian-style table!

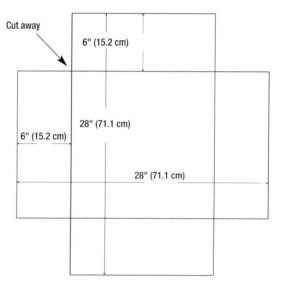

Step 2

Cut away

6" (15.2 cm)

6" (15.2 cm)

28" (71.1 cm)

28" (71.1 cm)

28" (71.1 cm) square

Oval Bird Art

How convenient that embroidery hoops are sold in oval shapes, with built-in hangers (use the screw to hang the hooped art).

Standing in line at a popular sandwich shop, I glanced upward at a sign that read "Please Order Here." It was silk-screened on canvas and ingeniously framed in an embroidery hoop. The following weekend, while attending an art opening at a friend's store, the same inventive framing made a second appearance. One artist showcased a provocative collection of surf-inspired fabric art, including woodblock prints on fabric scraps, in embroidery hoop frames! What a clever use for this traditional craft tool. These traditional George and Martha Washington silhouettes aren't quite as modern as this pair of hip blackbirds, comfortably perched in black embroidery hoops!

Old-fashioned framed silhouettes of George and Martha Washington

Instructions:

1. Spray-paint the embroidery hoops and let them dry.

2. Choose clip art from clip art books or the Internet, and photocopy or print the images onto transfer paper. The image will be backward unless you flip it.

3. Cut out the images.

4. Place the transfer paper face down on the right side of the fabric.

5. Press, following manufacturer's instructions. Use a press cloth to protect the iron.

6. Once the fabric is cool, carefully peel the paper backing from the image.

7. Insert the fabric with the newly transferred image between the two wood hoops, with the image centered and the hoop screw on the top.

8. Tighten the hoop screw and trim the excess fabric from the backside. Glue the edge of the fabric to the back of the hoop to hold it in place more securely.

9. Repeat for remaining hoop and image. (Reverse the direction of the second silhouette for a happy couple!)

10. Hang the embroidery hoops on the wall with a nail through the screw area.

Tools:

❋ Fabric glue
❋ Iron and ironing board
❋ Press cloth
❋ Scissors

Materials:

❋ Two 6" x 9" (15.2 x 22.9 cm) basswood oval embroidery hoops
❋ Two 12" x 12" (30.5 x 30.5 cm) pieces of white and black graphic fabric
❋ Black spray paint, glossy finish
❋ Silhouetted clip art of blackbirds or other motifs (from clip art books or online sources)
❋ Iron-on inkjet transfer paper
❋ Two nails

Flowerboxes

Cardboard storage containers are plain and boring, so make your own eye-catching arrangement of "flowerboxes"! Affix tranquil leaf- and stem-patterned fabric on the sides of each box and flower blossoms on the tops.

Flower boxes in the window delight in Geneva, Switzerland.

Fabric-covered storage boxes are perfect for safekeeping precious photos and mementos.

Tools:

❀ Foam brush
❀ Iron and ironing board
❀ Ruler
❀ Scissors

Materials:

❀ Craft storage boxes in different sizes (examples are 10" x 10" x 6" [25.4 x 25.4 x 15.2 cm], 8¾" x 8¾" x 4½" [22.3 x 22.3 x 11.4 cm], 8" x 8" x 4½" [20.3 x 20.3 x 10.2 cm])
❀ 1 yard (.9 m) "roots and stems" or other floral-patterned fabric, for bottoms of boxes
❀ ½ yard (.5 m) floral fabric, for appliqués
❀ Fabric Mod Podge
❀ Fabric glue
❀ Spray adhesive

Instructions:

1. Choose a fabric that has stems and leaves to cover the sides of the boxes.

2. Measure the height and circumference of the box without the lid on. Cut a strip of fabric 2½" (6.4 cm) greater than the box height and 1" (2.5 cm) longer than the circumference.

3. Press ¼" (6 mm) to wrong side along all long edges for a clean finish.

4. Spray adhesive on the wrong side of the fabric and center one side of the box on the fabric strip so there is 1" (2.5 cm) of fabric extending beyond the top and bottom of the box. Wrap the fabric around the box, smoothing it as you go and keeping it straight.

5. As you approach the end of the fabric strip, fold ⅞" (2.2 cm) under to form a clean edge where it meets the beginning of the strip. Add fabric glue to strengthen the area.

6. Fold the fabric to the bottom of the box. Press the sides to form mitered corners, much like wrapping the side panels of a gift box.

7. For the inside of the box, clip the fabric diagonally at the corners and press the fabric down into the box. If necessary, add fabric glue to hold the edges in place.

8. Cut large, whole flower motifs from the floral fabric and lay them out on the box lid until you are pleased with the arrangement. Repeat for remaining box lids.

9. Carefully brush Mod Podge directly onto the positioned fabric flowers with the foam brush (try to stay within the outlines of the flowers, since the glue will make the natural paper shiny).

10. Let your flowers dry and use the boxes to store your innocent bachelorette party Polaroids!

3

Crochet Beachcomber Rug

Made from strips of fabric, this laid-back crocheted rug brings the beach home.

A beachcomber is someone who combs the beach looking for the perfect spot where natural brown and soft white shells mingle with pale pink beach sand. This relaxed arrangement of shells and sand provides the inspiration for this laid-back, crocheted fabric rug. This project started off as a potholder and morphed into a fabulous patchwork rug. Cutting and pressing the fabric into workable strips changes the feel and characteristics of the fabric. Once all the fabric strips are joined the rug will be 37¼" wide x 28" (94.75 x 71 cm) long and it will be filled with charming flecks of color and imperfections as unique as beach sand.

This is a big project. If you prefer, start by crocheting a one-rectangle potholder or trivet, otherwise get ready to dive in, because you'll need to make 25 rectangles!

Seashells on the seashore

Tip: If your rug is going on a smooth surface such as tile or wood flooring, place a nonskid rug mat underneath it to prevent slipping.

Tools:

❋ Bias tape maker, ½" (12 mm)
❋ Crochet hook, size I/9 (5.5 mm) or size to obtain gauge
❋ Iron and ironing board
❋ Rotary cutter and cutting mat
❋ Ruler
❋ Sewing machine or sewing needle and thread
❋ Tapestry needle

Materials:

❋ 6¾ yds (6.25 m) 100% cotton fabric in pink/brown (A)
❋ 6 yds (5.5 m) 100% cotton fabric in tan (B)
❋ 6 yds (5.5 m) 100% cotton fabric in brown (C)
❋ 2½ yds (2.25 m) 100% cotton fabric in pink (D)

GAUGE:

❋ 10½ sc and 10½ rows = 4" (10 cm)

KEY:

❋ Ch – chain, sc – single crochet

Instructions:

1. Machine wash and dry the fabric. Press it to remove wrinkles. Cut the fabric into 1" (2.5 cm) -wide strips using a rotary cutter, cutting mat, and straight edge as a guide.

Tip: After the fabric is washed, cut strips lengthwise so they are longer, which means less sewing and a speedier process.

2. Place the short ends of two strips of the same color, with right sides together, at a right angle. Machine or hand sew the strips together diagonally. Continue sewing all the strips of one color together. Set them aside and repeat the process with the next color.

Step 2

Machine or hand sew strips together

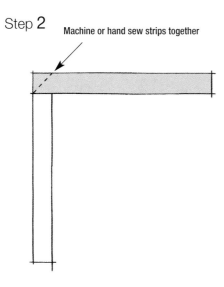

3. Iron the seams open and trim off the excess fabric.

Step 3

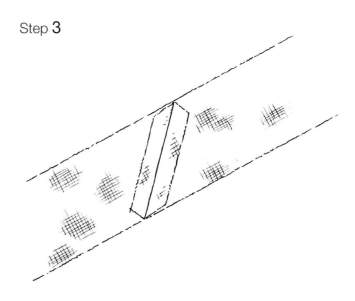

4. To create the fabric "yarn," insert the end of a strip into the bias tape maker. Use a steel crochet hook or pin to help pull the fabric through. The bias tape maker will automatically fold the fabric strip. Using a steam iron, press these folds to create a ½" (12 mm) strip. Slide the bias strip maker down the fabric and continue ironing the folds.

TO CROCHET RUG

5. For each rectangle, ch 20. Make 9 in A, 8 in B, and 8 in C.

> **Row 1 (Right Side):** Sc into 2nd ch from hook and in each ch across — 19 sc.
>
> **Rows 2 – 13:** Ch 1, turn, sc into each sc across. Fasten off. Steam press rectangles into shape.

6. Position finished rectangles on flat surface. Refer to the photograph or position them as you choose.

> **VERTICAL SEAM:** With fabric strip D and a slip knot (see page 144) on the hook, loosely sc the rectangles together. Begin with the first 2 rectangles in the bottom row. Hold them with wrong sides together, and matching row for row, sc through both pieces at the edge of each row. Don't cut the yarn; continue the seam by adding the first and second rectangles for the row above. Keep attaching the rectangles until there are five rows. Fasten off.
>
> Attach the third rectangles in each row to the second ones in the same way. Continue until all the rectangles are attached along the vertical edges.
>
> **HORIZONTAL SEAM:** Now attach the rows together in the same manner, but this time horizontally, working a sc into a vertical sc as you meet one when working across. Fasten off.

7. **Edging**–With fabric strip D and a slip knot on hook,

2 sc in top right corner of rug,

18 sc across to vertical seam,

*ch 2, skip vertical seam,

19 sc across next rectangle to vertical seam,

rep from * twice more,

ch 2, skip vertical seam,

18 sc across to top left corner,

3 sc in corner,

13 sc down left side of rectangle,

**ch 2, skip horizontal seam,

14 sc down left side to next horizontal seam,

rep from ** twice more,

ch 2, skip horizontal seam,

13 sc down left side of bottom left rectangle,

3 sc in corner,

18 sc across to vertical seam,

+ch 2, skip vertical seam,

19 sc across rectangle to next vertical seam,

rep from + twice more, ch 2,

skip vertical seam,

18 sc across to bottom right corner,

3 sc in corner,

13 sc up right side of rectangle,

#ch 2, skip horizontal seam,

14 sc up right side to next horizontal seam,

rep from # twice,

ch 2, skip horizontal seam,

13 sc up right side of top right rectangle,

sc in top right corner,

sl st into first sc to join.

8. With tapestry needle, weave ends into wrong side.

Linen Glow Ball

1

Inspiration comes from the strangest places!

Tip: Weave an electrical cord through the branches of a tree and hang several glow balls at different heights over your picnic table. You can use colored linens for more festive lanterns.

Crumpled discarded paper, lying next to your office trash bin (because you missed the basket while playing office basketball) can light up your life. This linen lantern exudes a casual quality with its semitranslucent, organic folds that look like warm sheets fresh out of the dryer. It is a juxtaposition of light and fabric, like that of Jasper Morrison's modern glow-ball light when it meets Christo and Jeanne-Claude's renowned fabric-wrapped trees project. Use this unique pendant as ambient lighting at your next outdoor soiree, and hang it from a tree in your backyard.

Even a crumpled ball of paper is worth a second glance.

Instructions:

1. Connect the 2 strands of white LED event lights by plugging one into the other. *This is the only type of bulb to use.*

2. Make a ball by winding the lights around themselves, as you might do with a ball of yarn. Hold the end that plugs into the outlet extended, and keep winding, until you have a tightly wound ball of lights.

3. Once you reach the last light on the string, tuck it into the ball and under a strand, and pull as tight as possible.

4. The ball of lights will hang by its cord, but you may need a white extension cord to add length to the pendant.

5. Put your light source aside and begin construction on the linen shade.

6. With the disappearing-ink fabric pen, draw a 24" (61 cm) -diameter circle in the center of the piece of linen. (See How to Draw a Circle, page 144.)

7. Zigzag stitch the edge of the circle to prevent fraying and press ¼" (6 mm) to the wrong side. Edge stitch along the folded edge.

8. Divide the perimeter of the fabric into twelfths, and mark it like the numbers on a clock. Make vertical (refer to sewing machine manual) buttonholes at the markings, ¼" (6 mm) from the edge. Wrap the fabric around the ball of lights and cinch it closed by threading a 12" (30.5 cm) piece of string through the buttonholes. Knot the string and hide it in the folds of the fabric.

9. To create the crumpled paper look, spray the linen with spray starch and randomly wrap the ball with string. Spray again. After the starch dries, remove the string. The wrinkles remain. (When have you ever wanted to keep wrinkles? How liberating!) Hang your glow ball at your next outdoor fete or place it on a bedside table for a warm indirect light.

Tools:

❀ Disappearing-ink fabric pen
❀ Sewing machine with buttonhole capabilities
❀ Sewing needle

Materials:

❀ 2 strands white LED wedding/party lights
❀ 30" (76.2 cm) square heavyweight white or ivory linen
❀ White or ivory thread
❀ ¼" (6 mm) -diameter cotton string
❀ Spray starch

Mod-ern Tasseled Shade

Tip: Raise the shade to its highest position, and measure how long the new shaped piece needs to be so that it is visible below the folds of the shade. Our shaped bottom is 12" (30.5 cm) long, but only 5" (12.7 cm) is visible when the shade is drawn up.

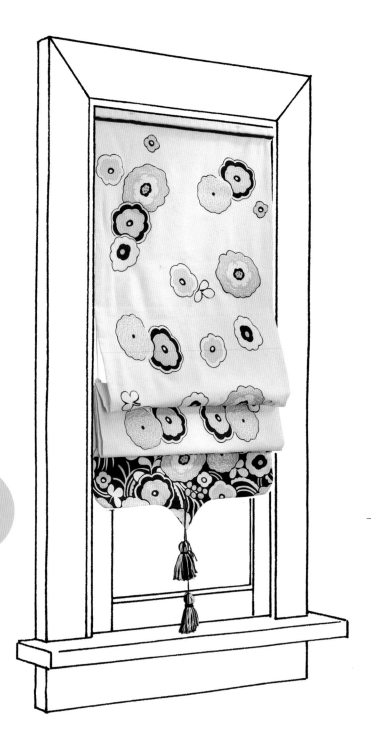

A classic retro black, yellow, and white print from Marimekko has awesome, visual impact.

Tools:

* Craft paper
* Iron and ironing board

OPTIONAL:

* Glue gun and glue sticks
* Press cloth
* Sewing machine with buttonhole capabilities
* Scissors
* Zipper foot
* Cardboard 4" x 6" (10.2 x 15.2 cm)

Materials:

FOR WINDOW 24" (61 CM) WIDE:

* Natural canvas Roman shade (width to fit your window)
* 1.5 yards (1.4 m) mod retro black, yellow, and white fabric
* Paper-backed fusible web
* Yarn or string in white and black (you can also add gold for sparkle)
* 24" (61 cm) black ribbon or trim

Mod and modern, this stylish color combination is seen everywhere from Kelly Werstler's hip hotels to Jonathan Adler's quirky home collection. Revive the 1960s with this groovy window shade and do it the easy way, with a ready-made canvas Roman shade. Simply embellish the bottom with a burst of pattern and color. Don't throw away the scraps; use them as flower power on the body of the shade. If you prefer, start from scratch and make your own Roman shade. (See Belted Safari Shade on page 50.)

Use a pre-made roman shade, and add some flower power for mod results!

Instructions:

1. Design the shape you would like to add to the bottom of a pre-made Roman shade, or refer to the pattern shown on page 158. Enlarge the pattern on a photo copy machine to the desired size to fit your window. This pattern is designed for a 24" (61 cm) wide window and includes ½" (1.3 cm) seam allowance.

2. Trace your own design, or the template provided, onto craft paper and use it to cut two pieces of fabric. Cut each piece with the template on the fold of the fabric.

3. With right sides together, sew the two pieces together on the bottom and sides with ½" (1.3 cm) seam. Leave the top open.

4. Turn the shaped piece right side out and press.

5. Press the top edges ½" (1.3 cm) to the wrong side and slide them over the bottom of the shade. Pin to secure in place.

6. Stitch straight, with a zipper foot, across the bottom of the shade, through all the layers, catching the top of the shaped piece on both the front and back of the shade.

IF YOU DESIRE A FIELD OF FLOWERS AND THEN SOME...

OPTIONAL: If you wish, and the fabric is suitable, cut several floral motifs (with extra fabric all around) from the fabric.

7. Following manufacturer's instructions, fuse paper-backed fusible web onto the back of the floral motifs.

8. Now trim around the perimeter of the motifs exactly as you want them to appear on the shade. Peel away the paper backing from the fusible web. Iron the motifs onto the shade. Use a press cloth between the fabric and the iron.

9. Glue a length of ribbon trim across the top of the shade with a glue gun.

TO MAKE THE TASSEL, KEEP GOING...

OPTIONAL: To make a 4" (10.2 cm) tassel, cut a piece of cardboard 4" x 6" (10.2 x 15.2 cm).

10. Place a piece of yarn across the top of the cardboard.

11. Wind the yarn around the center of the cardboard, over the string. Add a second color yarn if you want a two-tone tassel.

12. Continue winding the yarn until it is desired thickness for a tassel.

13. Tie the ends of the top string into a tight knot.

14. Cut open the bottom loops at the bottom of the cardboard and remove the cardboard.

15. Tie a short length of yarn around the tassel about 1.5" (3.8 cm) from the top in a knot and tuck the ends into the tassel. This creates the ball at the top of the tassel.

16. Trim the ends of the tassel so they are all the same length.

17. Repeat to make one more tassel. Tie the tassels together with a long length of yarn that runs through the top of each tassel.

18. Make a buttonhole (refer to sewing machine manual) in the center of the shaped piece and feed the tassel through the buttonhole for added drama!

19. Install the shade in the window following the instructions that came with the shade.

Suburban Landscape Silk Quilt and Shams

Fact: In the 1960s, United States president Eisenhower supported the integration of the national highway system, which linked county and state roads across the country. Before then, things moved a lot slower; you had to drive from town to town to get to where you wanted to go.

Unexpected fabric choices make everyday bedding unique!

ere's a project where the designer embraced textiles as a canvas for uninhibited, graphic experimentation. Congested highways and banal, everyday sights become fresh and exciting when transformed into textiles and mixed with other fabrics. The cul-de-sac fabric is inspired by common residential land plots as seen from above and the fabric that looks like Celtic knots and Ottoman tile work is, in fact, a bird's-eye view of our highway system! Offbeat fabric selection is all it takes to turn a mundane-looking bed into something spectacular. Instructions are for a queen-size bed quilt, 86" x 86" (218.4 x 218.4 cm). If you are short on time, make the flanged pillow shams instead. Change the width of the pleated strips, the mixing of fabric patterns, and even the color of the fabric for a few extra pillow shams and for a collage of color and pattern.

A sprawling suburban spread!

Tools:

* Disappearing-ink fabric pen
* Iron and ironing board
* Pins
* Press cloth
* Sewing machine
* Scissors
* Tape measure

Materials:

* Photograph shows 2 coordinating prints and 1 solid silk dupioni or silk broadcloth, 45" wide (114.3cm)

FOR BED QUILT:

* 2 yards (1.8 m) print fabric for center panel (A)
* 3 yards (2.7 m) coordinating print fabric for sides and center bottom panel (B)
* 2½" yards (2.3 m) solid fabric for quilted panels (C)
* 2½" yards (2.3) of 108" (2.7 m) -wide quilt back fabric or 5 yards (4.6 m) of 45" (114.3 cm) wide fabric
* 2½" yards (2.3) of 108" (2.7 m) -wide white quilter's flannel
* Thread to match solid color fabric and fabric B

FOR ONE PILLOW SHAM:

* Use remnants from the quilt, or ¾ yard (1.9 cm) print fabric (A)
* ¼ yard (22.9 mm) coordinating print fabric (B)
* ¼ yard (6 mm) solid fabric (C)
* ¾ yard (1.9 cm) backing fabric (D)
* ¼ yard (6 mm) white quilter's flannel
* Thread to match solid color fabric and print fabric
* Pillow insert 20" x 26" (50.8 x 66 cm)

Instructions:

INSTRUCTIONS FOR BED QUILT:

Use ½" (1.3 cm) seam allowance at all times, and a press cloth when pressing silk fabric.

CUTTING INSTRUCTIONS:

Fabric A   (Cut 1) 39" x 66" (99.1 x 167.4 cm)

Fabric B   (Cut 1) 14" x 39" (35.6 x 99.1 cm)
                (Cut 2) 19½" x 89" (49.5 x 226 cm)

Fabric C   (Cut 1) 11" x 39 (27.9 x 99.1 cm)
                (Cut 2) 9" x 89" (22.9 x 226 cm)

Fabric D   (Cut 1) 86" x 86" (218.4 x 218.4 cm)

Quilter's flannel (Cut 1) 86" x 86" (218.4 x 218.4 cm)
(piece fabric if necessary)

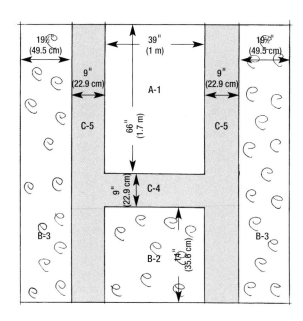

Cutting Layout

QUILT FRONT

Cut fabric as indicated.
Refer to illustration for piece numbers.

1. To make the center panel, sew piece 1 to piece 4 with right sides together. Sew the other side of piece 4 to piece 2, as shown in the photograph on page 106. Press.

2. With right sides together, sew each piece 5 to the side edges of the center panel. Press.

3. With right sides together, sew each piece 3 to each piece 5. Press. This completes the top of the quilt and it should measure 92" wide (233.7 cm) and 89" long (226 cm).

4. To join the layers, place the wrong side of the quilt top over the quilter's flannel and loosely pin the fabrics together.

5. Stitch in the ditch (see page 144) up the side of each vertical solid panel and along the top and bottom of the horizontal solid panel using matching top thread (mild puckering is acceptable).

6. Pin the wrong side of the quilt bottom to the back of the quilter's flannel, with pins approximately every 6" to 10" (15.2 to 25.4 cm) across the entire quilt.

7. Sew parallel rows of top stitching on all solid-color panels. Starting in the middle of the left solid panel, topstitch from top to bottom, removing pins as you stitch.

8. Alternating between the left and right of the first stitched line, topstitch from top to bottom (remove pins as you stitch) every ½" (1.3 cm). (Don't worry; the puckering occurs naturally.)

Tip: The top thread color should match the top fabric and bobbin thread color should match the bottom fabric.

9. Repeat steps 7 and 8 for right solid panel and for the solid color horizontal panel.

10. To bind the edges, press the raw edges of the top of the quilt under ½" (1.3 cm) on all sides. Put your quilt face down on a wide, flat surface. (The floor or dining table covered with sheets is a good option.)

11. Starting with the top and bottom edges, fold 1" (2.5 cm) to the back of the quilt to cover the edges of the backing and flannel fabric. Pin.

12. Fold and pin the side edges 2½" (6.4 cm) to the back of the quilt to cover the edges of the backing and flannel fabric.

Steps 11 & 12

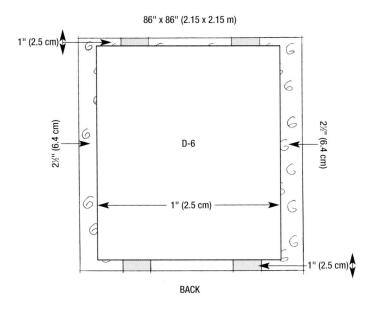

86" x 86" (2.15 x 2.15 m)

1" (2.5 cm)

2½" (6.4 cm)

D-6

2½" (6.4 cm)

1" (2.5 cm)

1" (2.5 cm)

BACK

13. Press all sides and neaten corners.

14. To finish the quilt, and so you cannot see your stitches, sew with the back of the quilt up. Change the thread so you use the backing color thread in the needle and the quilt face color thread in the bobbin. Edge stitch close to the folded edge of the quilt front (which is now folded to the back of the quilt). Sew four separate seams, so you secure the corners.

INSTRUCTIONS FOR PILLOW SHAM:
24" x 32" (61 x 81.3 cm)

(½" [1.3 cm] seam allowance at all times, use a press cloth when pressing silk fabric)

CUTTING INSTRUCTIONS:

Fabric C (Cut 1) 7" x 27" (17.8 x 68.6 cm)

Fabric A (Cut 2) 10" x 27" (25.4 x 68.6 cm)

Fabric B (Cut 2) 4" x 25" (49.5 x 63.5 cm)

Fabric D –Pillow sham back (Cut 2) 25" x 20½" (63.5 x 52.1 cm)

Quilter's flannel (Cut 1) 7 " x 27" (17.8 x 68.6 cm)

SCHEMATIC FOR SHAM FRONT

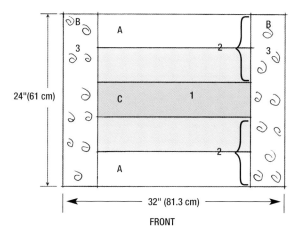

FRONT

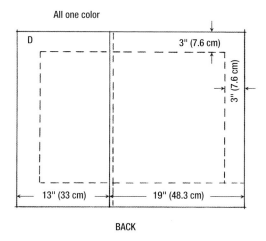

All one color

BACK

1. Cut the fabric as indicated. Refer to the illustration for piece numbers. Place piece 1 over quilter's flannel with right side up, pin all over.

2. Starting in the middle of the panel, topstitch from top to bottom through both layers (remove pins as you stitch).

3. Alternating between the left and right of the first stitched line, repeat step 2 every ½" (1.3 cm). (Don't worry—the puckering occurs naturally).

4. With right sides together, sew pieces 2 to each long side of piece 1. Press seams away from center panel. Zigzag or overlock seams for a cleaner finish.

5. With right sides together, sew pieces 3 to the sides the pieced center panel. (See photograph, page 106.) Press and zigzag or overlock seams.

6. To create the envelope enclosure in the back, finish one 25" (63.5 cm) end of each back piece, by folding under ½" (1.3 cm) and then ½" (1.3 cm) again to the wrong side. Press and edge stitch close to the folded edge.

7. With right sides up, lay the right back piece over the left back piece, so it overlaps by 6" (15.2 cm). Now only 13½" (34.3 cm) of the left back piece is visible. Pin, and sew the top and bottom edges to keep the two fabrics together. (You should have a rectangle with an overlapping slit for inserting the pillow.)

8. To finish the sham, pin the top (pieced silk) and bottom (overlapping pieces) with right sides together and sew around all the edges. Press and trim corner seam allowances.

9. Turn the pillow sham right side out and poke out the corners so that they form sharp 90 degree angles. Press flat and pin the pieces together around the edges.

10. Measure and pin mark 3" (7.6 cm) from all outside edges and top stitch around the entire pillow sham to create the flange. Make your bed!

Citrus Placemats and Coasters

Fresh from the grove, these table accessories are sweet and juicy!

To this day, my mom still uses the same plastic-laminated placemats that I remember seeing under my bowl of Fruity Pebbles cereal when I was growing up. Citrus fruits printed on white vinyl danced under my morning meals. Ever since my parents moved back into my childhood home, a trip to visit them is a trip back in time, and an infinite source of inspiration. I couldn't get my mom to part with even one of our special placemats (or maybe I was embarrassed to show you how worn it had gotten) for photography. So, the vibrant colors of assorted citrus fruits are now the inspiration for these summertime placemats and coasters. Oilcloth is the perfect surface fabric because it can be wiped clean with a damp cloth. To give the placemat cushioning and to help it grip the table, we glued it to fun foam (a popular kids' craft product).

Juicy citrus fruits taste and look like summer.

Instructions:

INSTRUCTIONS FOR 12" X 18" (30.5 X 45.7 CM) PLACEMATS AND 4" X 4" (10.2 X 10.2 CM) COASTERS:

1. Cut four pieces of placemat oilcloth slightly larger than the foam sheets.

2. Spray adhesive on one side of a foam sheet; coat the edges a little extra. Carefully place the foam sheet with the adhesive side down, in the center of the wrong side of one of the pieces of oilcloth. Let the adhesive dry.

3. Use the craft knife and a metal straightedge to cut around the edges of the oilcloth so the edges align perfectly with the foam sheet. Repeat with remaining three pieces of cut oilcloth.

4. Cut the coordinating oilcloth to cover the remaining foam sheet and follow steps 2 and 3.

5. Cut 4" (10.2 cm) squares for coasters from this last foam sheet.

6. Serve up a fruit salad and pour some lemonade!

Tools:

❀ Craft knife and cutting mat
❀ Metal ruler
❀ Scissors

Materials:

❀ 1 yard (.9 m) oilcloth fabric for 4 placemats
❀ ⅓ yard (30.5 cm) coordinating oilcloth fabric for 4–12 drink coasters
❀ 5 sheets 12" x 18" (30.5 cm x 45.7 cm) foam
❀ Spray adhesive

Happy Homemaker Dishtowels

Colorful handmade dishtowels add kitsch to your kitchen.

Tip: For the appliqué, look for fabrics that have defined animals, flowers, or other graphics that are easy to cut out. Use pinking shears for an amusing zigzag edge.

Betty Crocker baking kits were my first introduction to cooking; everything you needed to make delicious goodies in one box! I loved making cupcakes for the monthly bake sale at my elementary school, probably because I got to mix and match gobs of frosting and sprinkles to decorate each cupcake and make each one special, just like these dishtowels. It was a time when kitchen kitsch was cool. The stainless-steel, Caloric brand (I've never heard of it either) wall oven that my mother still uses today reminds me of a 1950s pickup truck. Next to it, on the white Formica counter, sat a pink polar bear ceramic pitcher.

Create these cheerful dishtowels, in contrasting bright hues, as a throwback to a time when it was cool to have kitschy kitchen flair. A yard of fabric makes two towels, each 21" x 31" (53.3 x 78.7 cm).

Stop by for a piece of pie at Café Kitsch.

Instructions:

1. Cut dishtowel fabric into pieces 22" x 32" (55.9 x 81.3 cm).

2. Press ¼" (6 mm) to the wrong side and then ¼" (6 mm) again, on all four sides. Edge stitch close to the inside fold.

3. Cut a single motif or a group of motifs from the appliqué fabric. Leave 2" (5.1 cm) around all sides.

4. Fuse the paper-backed adhesive onto the back of the motifs, following the manufacturer's instructions. Use a press cloth to protect the iron.

5. Trim close to the motif(s) with pinking shears, and then position it (them) on the lower right side of the dishtowel.

6. Remove the paper backing and fuse the motif in place, as in step 4.

7. Cut trim 22" (55.9 cm) long and fold ½" (1.3 cm) to the back at each edge. Pin the trim along the bottom of the towel, either with the heading on the right side of the towel so it is part of the décor, or on the wrong side of the towel, so the pompons hang below the hem.

8. Topstitch the trim across the top and bottom long edges of the heading.

9. Hang your finished dishtowels in the kitchen for cheerful cleanups.

Tools:

* Iron and ironing board
* Pinking shears
* Pins
* Press cloth
* Scissors
* Sewing machine

Materials:

* 1 yard (.9 m) each of two different graphic, machine-washable fabrics
* ⅓" yard (.3 m) contrasting fabric for appliqués (or piece large enough to cut complete appliqué)
* 1 yard (.9 m) of pompon trim
* Paper-backed fusible adhesive
* Thread

Antler Trophy Pillow

Show off your prize and make up a hunting story from the comfort of your couch!

Whether or not you're a hunter, classic lodge décor is appealing in a rugged, country-cabin kind of way. Let this velvet trophy satisfy your quest for buck antlers in the form of a three-dimensional, fuzzy pillow. It's just the thing for that favorite armchair in your moose-country hunting lodge.

It's hard to deny the magnificence of a young buck with fearsome antlers.

Instructions:

1. Enlarge the pillow pattern and antler appliqué 200% on a photocopier machine. (See Templates, page 159.)

2. Cut two pillow pattern pieces of brown velvet and one antler appliqué of ivory bouclé.

3. Pin the antler appliqué in the center of one of the brown velvet pieces and invisibly slipstitch it around all edges. (See Slipstitch, page 142.)

4. Use embroidery floss to accent the edges of the antler appliqué with periodic cross stitches. (See How to Cross Stitch, page 143.)

5. With right sides together, sew the two pillow pieces together, leaving a 3" (7.6 cm) opening on one side. Clip the curved seam allowance and trim the corners and points.

6. Turn the pillow right side out and stuff it with fiberfill to desired thickness. Be sure to push fiberfill into the pointed areas.

7. Slipstitch the opening closed.

8. Place the pillow on the sofa and brag about your latest trophy.

Tools:

❄ Hand sewing needle
❄ Pins
❄ Scissors
❄ Sewing machine

Materials:

❄ ½ yard (45 cm) brown velvet
❄ 12" x 12" (30.5 x 30.5 cm) piece of ivory bouclé fabric
❄ Thread
❄ Chartreuse embroidery floss
❄ Polyester fiberfill

2

Perforated Ultrasuede Café Curtain

A modern material meets a conventional window treatment.

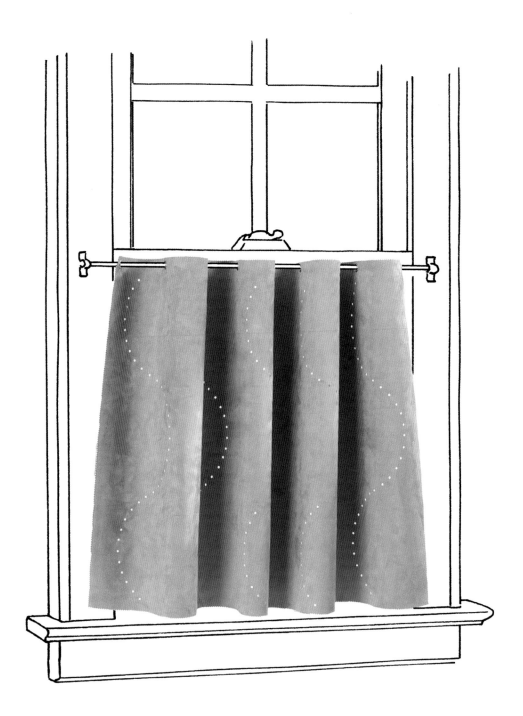

The punched hole detailing on this modern-looking window treatment is inspired by nature's own sea urchin. Holes punched in Ultrasuede (which doesn't fray) create a quick and easy way to embellish and hang a simple café curtain. Ultrasuede is durable, easy to clean, and it looks and feels like expensive suede. It's no surprise that interior designers use it liberally, and so can you. This curtain hangs over the lower half of the window to provide privacy. Sunlight streams in through the top half of the window and the perforated design of this contemporary window treatment.

Look at the ingenious patterning of dots on the sea urchin's shell.

Tip: If you have trouble punching the grommet through your fabric, start by cutting a small x in the correct spot with a utility knife.

Tools:

❁ Craft paper (optional)
❁ Disappearing-ink fabric pen
❁ Grommet tools
❁ Hole punch set for leather or paper (example uses a 5 mm hole)
❁ Piece of scrap wood for support
❁ Pinking shears
❁ Yardstick

Materials:

❁ Ultrasuede (for yardage to fit your window, see step 1)
❁ ¾" (1.9 cm) silver grommets (enough to span width of curtain)
❁ ⅜" (1 cm) wood dowel or metal rod equal to width of window (diameter less than grommet diameter)
❁ Silver spray paint (for wood dowel only)

Instructions:

1. This is a café curtain that hangs across the lower half of the window. Mark the desired position of the hanging rod and measure from that marking. Seam allowance is not necessary, because Ultrasuede doesn't fray.

> **MEASUREMENTS:**
> **LENGTH** = from hanging rod to sill
> **WIDTH** = 1½ x distance across window

2. Use a yardstick and disappearing-ink fabric pen to draw straight cutting lines equal to the desired measurements. Cut along the cutting lines with pinking shears for a decorative edge.

3. Measure and mark grommet locations at each corner and at even intervals (about every 6½" [16.5 cm]) between the corners.

4. Apply grommets, following manufacturer's instructions.

5. To create a perforated pattern, cut a piece of craft paper the same size as the curtain and design the pattern on paper first. Use the disappearing-ink fabric pen to draw the pattern on the wrong side of the fabric.

6. Place a piece of wood under the Ultrasuede for support and punch holes with the hole punch, following the marked pattern.

7. Paint the wooden dowel silver or use a metal rod.

8. Hang the brackets to support the dowel/rod.

9. Insert the dowel/rod through the grommets and hang the curtain as planned.

10. Stand back and admire!

DIFFICULTY RATING
1

Fresh Fabric Vases

Tip: Be careful when filling flower vases with water so that the fabric does not get wet.

Decorate cylinders with fabric for dramatic flower vases or captivating candle lanterns.

Bubble wrap has a thankless job protecting precious and fragile items but it has always been visually interesting to me with its modern grid of dimensional dots. I came across a fabric that actually resembles bubble wrap and in just a few minutes, these fabric vases were born. Wrap fabric (semi-transparent fabric or thin lace cloth work great) around glass cylinders to make elegant fresh flower vases or candle lanterns. These three vases, all different sizes, are covered with a variety of materials, textures, and colors to create a random collection. Each is banded on the top and bottom with chocolate brown ribbon for cohesiveness. Fabric selection is a matter of preference; choose elegant fabric for a special celebration or more casual fabrics for informal fun!

Everyone wants to pop Bubble Wrap, which is
appealing visually and to the touch.

Instructions:

1. Measure the height and circumference of the cylinder. Add 1" (2.5 cm) to the circumference measurement and cut a piece of fabric to those measurements.

2. Spray adhesive lightly and uniformly around the outside of the cylinder

3. With cut edges even with the top and bottom of the cylinder, wrap the fabric around, smoothing it and making sure the edges remain aligned. The fabric will overlap the beginning edge by 1" (2.5 cm).

4. If the fabric frays, fold the overlap edge ¼" (6 mm) to the wrong side and glue it in place with the glue gun. If the over lap edge doesn't fray or it has an interesting pattern, just glue it flat to cover the beginning edge.

5. Use the glue gun to affix ribbon around the top and bottom of the cylinder, over the fabric edges.

6. Repeat for remaining cylinders.

7. Fill the closed-bottom cylinders with fresh flowers, or place candles under open ones to make candle hurricanes.

Fact: Bubble Wrap was an accident, created by a pair of engineers in 1957. They were trying to create a textured plastic wallpaper with paper backing that could be easily cleaned.

Tools:

❀ Disappearing-ink fabric pen
❀ Glue gun and glue sticks
❀ Scissors
❀ Spray adhesive
❀ Tape measure

Materials:

❀ Three glass cylinders of different sizes (with a bottom to hold water and flowers, bottomless for candles)
❀ Three ¼ yard (22.9 cm) pieces of different fabrics, sheer or semi-transparent fabrics work well (see Resources, page 146)
❀ ⅜" (1 cm) ribbon (circumference of cylinder x 2 = yardage for that cyclinder)
❀ Fresh flowers or candles

2

Suede Squares Rug

Tools:

❉ Iron and ironing board
❉ Leather sewing machine needle
❉ Press cloth
❉ Scissors
❉ Sewing machine

Fact: Scraps of fabric are easier to come by. Is it a coincidence or not? Patchwork appears to be the trendy method designers in this book used to create rugs! (See Patchwork Taxidermy Animal Rug on page 28 and Crochet Beachcomber Rug on page 98.)

Materials:

❉ Twelve 12" x 12" (30.5 x 30.5 cm) squares of suede, different colors optional
❉ 39" x 51" (99.1 x 129.5 cm) piece of natural-colored painter's canvas
❉ Matching thread
❉ 36" x 48" (91.4 x 121.9 cm) fusible tricot interfacing
❉ Spray adhesive

Tip: You can use fabric other than suede; however, if it frays, cut the squares 13" x 13" (33 x 33 cm) and fold ½" (1.3 cm) to the wrong side on all sides. Edge stitch close to the fold.

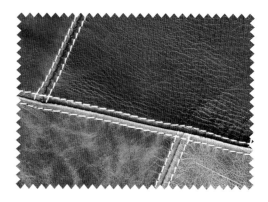

My design studio is in an industrial loft in downtown Manhattan. The building is filled with artists and creative individuals. (Several of the designers in this book are neighbors.) We all share a spot in the entrance hall, where we deposit our unwanted materials, knowing they have the potential to be another's treasure. On more than one occasion, I've exited my elevator to find a material morsel just waiting to be picked up and shaped into another form. One day, I found suede sample squares from a high-end leather manufacturer. The squares reminded me of patchwork leather, popular in 1970s; fortunately these were in beautiful, muted colors. Stitching the squares onto a background of neutral painter's canvas made a smart-looking accent rug. Notice the grommets that were in the squares when I found them; they add an air of recycled authenticity!

Leather patchwork with contrast stitching has retro style.

Boogie down with a funky patchwork rug made from leather samples.

Instructions:

1. Lay out the precut suede (or hemmed fabric) squares right side up on the fusible interfacing to plan color/pattern placement. With sides abutting, fuse them in place, following manufacturer's instructions.

2. Spray the canvas with spray adhesive, and center the fused suede squares on top with a 1½" (3.8 cm) border all around.

3. Topstitch the squares to the canvas across the length and width of the entire grid. (Check to make sure you've stitched down all sides of every square.)

Step 1

1½" (3.8 cm)   Stitch

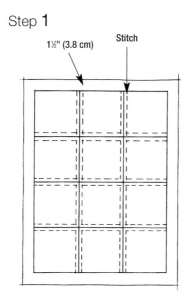

4. Press ½" (1.3 cm) of the canvas to the right side on all four sides. Press the remaining 1" (2.5 cm) toward the right side to encase the edges. This forms a 1" (2.5 cm) canvas border on the right side of the rug.

5. Form miters on all four corners. (See How to Form a Mitered Corner on page 145)

   NOTE: For this project, press and sew the hem to the right side, not to the wrong side, as in the instructions on page 145.

6. Edge stitch the border along the pressed edge to finish.

Step 4

1" (2.5 cm)

1" (2.5 cm)   1" (2.5 cm)

1" (2.5 cm)

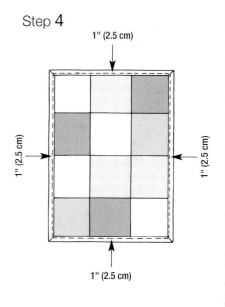

Trompe l'Oeil Pendant Lamp

Don't throw it out—look at a white wicker basket in a new light!

A scalloped and layered luxe window treatment is multi-dimensional and elegant as it softly filters light.

Tools:

❀ Drill
❀ Glue gun and glue sticks
❀ Ruler
❀ Scissors
❀ Sewing machine

Materials:

❀ Wicker wastebasket
❀ White spray paint, glossy finish (optional)
❀ 1 yard (.9 m) black and white fabric with graphic pattern
❀ ¼ yard (22.9 cm) complementary fabric for cord cover
❀ Thread
❀ Electrical socket with cord
❀ Metal hanging loop or chain
❀ Lightbulb

Create an optical illusion by draping and gluing strips of fabric to an old (but rejuvenated) wicker container. The project designer found common inspiration in the scalloped window treatment and the black and white fabric she chose for this project. The fabric pattern lends itself to the outlines of the window shade, which appear to scallop and trick the eye into believing it is three-dimensional, when in actuality, it's flat. The contrast of black on white is *très chic*! The open pattern of wicker, covered with overlapping strips of fabric, radiates a soft, diffused, and enchanting light.

Instructions:

1. Find/buy/recycle a wicker bathroom-sized trashcan.

2. Drill a hole in the center of the bottom of the trashcan. The hole should equal the diameter of the plug, plus a little extra, so you can thread the plug through the hole.

3. Spray trashcan with spray paint (if necessary). Let dry.

4. Examine your fabric. Cut one strip of fabric equal to the circumference of the top of the trashcan and about 6" (15.2 cm) wide (scallop one edge if you like the look of the example). Cut out the graphic motifs or create your own shape using the pattern of the fabric. The fabric we used had an obvious scalloped pattern. If you prefer, use the half-circle pattern provided to create a scalloped pattern with your fabric. (See Templates, page 160.)

5. Turn the trashcan upside down and wrap the strip around the open end. Hot glue it in place as you wrap.

6. Continue wrapping and gluing staggered layers of fabric to cover the trashcan.

7. Thread the electrical cord through the hole, from inside the trashcan, and then through the metal hanging loop, so that the socket is in the trashcan and the hanging loop extends out of the hole.

8. Cut two pieces of cord-cover fabric, each 4½" (11.4 cm) wide and a long as the width of the fabric. Sew the short ends with right sides together to make one long strip. Fold the strip in half lengthwise with right sides together. Measure and mark 4" (10.2 cm) from one end.

9. Begin seaming the fabric to form a tube with ½" (1.3 cm) seam allowance. When you reach the 4" (10.2 cm) mark, gradually make the seam allowance larger in order to make the tube narrower. Eventually the seam allowance should be 1½" (3.8 cm) so the tube is much narrower.

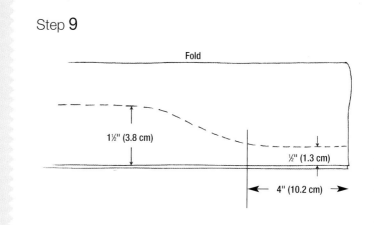

Step 9

Fold

1½" (3.8 cm)

½" (1.3 cm)

4" (10.2 cm)

10. Trim away excess seam allowance. Turn the tube right side out and press.

11. Slide the fabric tube over the chain and scrunch it down for a ruched effect. Hot glue the wider end to the trashcan, making sure the hanging loop is outside the fabric tube.

12. Insert a lightbulb into the socket.

13. Hang the lamp from a hook in the ceiling, and let the covered cord swag over to the outlet.

Super Strapping Wall Organizer

It clings to your wall and collects the mail with modern style

Tools:

❋ Leather sewing machine needle
❋ Tailor's chalk
❋ Scissors
❋ Sewing machine
❋ Yardstick

Materials:

❋ ¾ yard (1.9 cm) 54" (137.1 cm) heavy-weight fabric, such as canvas or faux leather
❋ 6 yards (5.5 m) 1" (2.5 cm) wide nylon strapping
❋ 2 flat wooden dowels or metal rods, 1" wide x 24" long (2.5 x 61 cm)
❋ 2 D-rings
❋ Contrasting thread

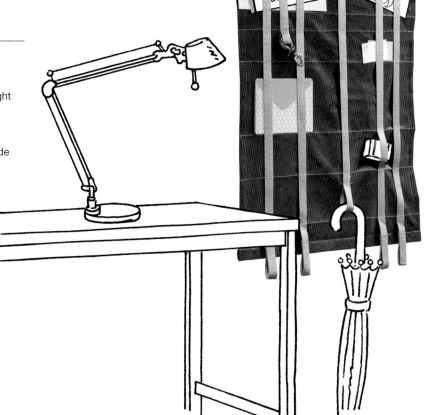

Dorothee Maurer-Becker, for Ingo Maurer, designed the super-groovy Utensilo wall organizer in 1970.

Motivated by the need to get organized and by a fun retro wall storage unit, we created our very own strapping wall organizer from fabric and common belting material. It hugs the wall and holds your things! The modern, vertical lines make it just the thing for collecting mail, leaving notes for your roommate, holding your umbrella, or acting as the backdrop for a rotating picture show. The organizer shown here is 24" x 43" (61 x 109.2 cm), but you can make yours any size.

Instructions:

1. Cut your fabric so it is 26" x 47" (66 x 119.4 cm).

2. Fold 1" (2.5 cm) to the wrong side on each side and 2" (5.1 cm) to the wrong side on the bottom. If the fabric ravels, first press ¼" (6 mm) to the wrong side to create a finished edge. Topstitch side and bottom hems close to inner hem fold.

3. Cut nylon strapping the following measurements (or any measurements to suit your needs): four pieces each 51" (129.5 cm), one piece 45" (114.3 cm), one piece 26" (66 cm), and one piece 15" (38.1 cm).

4. Sew the edge of each strapping piece to the top edge of the organizer. See the illustration for suggested placement.

5. Slide a D-ring on the two outside strapping pieces up to the top.

6. Fold the top edge, including the strapping 2" (5.1 cm) to the wrong side, and stitch across the width of the fabric panel 1½" (3.8 cm) from the folded edge. Be sure to hold strapping straight and catch each strap in the seam. Refer to the photograph.

7. Use tailor's chalk (check that markings disappear, or work on the wrong side) and a yardstick to draw stitching guidelines across the fabric panel. Refer to illustration for suggested placement of stitching lines.

8. Sew across the guidelines, catching the strapping in the stitching, and then sew directly over previous stitching for extra strength.

9. Fold the ends of each strapping under to create the desired size loops and top stitch the ends in place, or catch the ends in the horizontal stitching. Sew across the ends of the loops a few times, for greater strength.

10. Slide the metal bar or flat wood dowel into the top and bottom pockets.

11. Hang the organizer on a wall in your home office or by your front door to collect the mail.

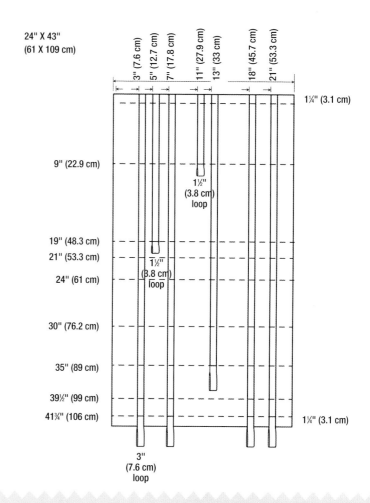

iPillow

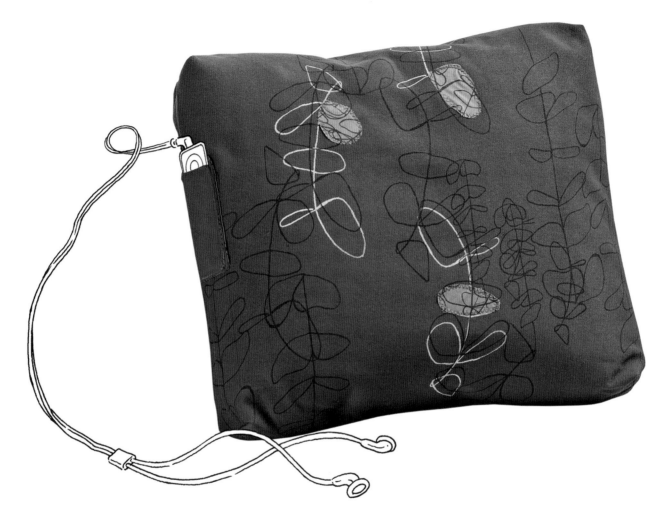

A lounging pillow for your iPod...and for you!

If you've kept up with the trend in gadgets and aren't stuck with that '80s tape deck-Walkman combo, then you're probably spending much of your transit time, and even your downtime, with an Ipod attached to your ears.

Recently, my cousin gave me an Ipod to replace my archaic portable CD player. It's an item you can't help but accessorize, as I did the day after I got it, with silicone covers in multiple colors, a connector for the car, a dock for the office, and a clip to wear it at the gym. Have you ever fallen asleep with your Ipod, only to wake up with it dangling dangerously close to the floor? Make this Ipillow and you'll have a happy place to take a snooze with your little friend.

Go ahead and take a snooze.

Tools:

❀ Disappearing-ink fabric pen

❀ Iron and ironing board

❀ Pins

❀ Ruler

❀ Scissors

❀ Sewing machine

Materials:

❀ ⅔ yard (.6 m) 45" (114.3 cm) -wide fabric

❀ 16" x 16" (40.6 x 40.6 cm) pillow form

❀ Matching thread

Instructions:

1. Machine wash, dry, and iron the fabric. Cut five pieces the following measurements:

> **One rectangle**
> 42" x 17" (106.7 x 43.2 cm) for main pillow
>
> **Two rectangles**
> 3½" x 4½" (8.9 x 11.4 cm) for lower iPod pocket
>
> **Two rectangles**
> 2¼" x 4¼" (5.7 x 10.8 cm) for top pocket

2. Hem the short ends of the main pillow piece by pressing ¼" (6 mm) to the wrong side, and then ¼" (6 mm) again. Stitch close to the folded edge.

3. Draw a line 12" (30.5 cm) in from each hemmed edge with the disappearing ink pen, and mark pocket location, 9½" (24.1 cm) over from the left hemmed edge and 5" (12.7 cm) down from the top edge.

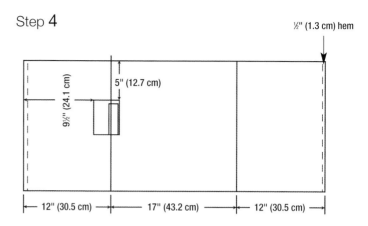

Schematic of Measurements

Step 4

½" (1.3 cm) hem

9½" (24.1 cm)

5" (12.7 cm)

12" (30.5 cm)   17" (43.2 cm)   12" (30.5 cm)

4. Sew both iPod pockets. Stitch same size pocket pieces together, with right sides facing with ½" (1.3 cm) seam allowance around all four sides, leaving an opening to turn pocket right side out. Trim corners diagonally and turn pockets right side out.

5. Press pockets. Turn unstitched seam allowances to the inside and edge stitch the opening closed.

6. Pin smaller pocket (stitched edge on top) to the right side of the larger pocket so sides and bottoms align and top edge of smaller pocket is slightly below top edge of larger pocket. Edge stitch sides and bottom of pocket in place. Back stitch at beginning and end of seam.

7. Pin larger pocket onto main fabric at marking with stitched edge across the top. Edge stitch sides and bottom through all layers. Back stitch at beginning and end of seam.

8. Fold main fabric piece at marked lines, with right sides together so that hemmed edges overlap.

9. Sew across the top and bottom through all layers with ½" (1.3 cm) seam allowance.

10. Before turning the pillow right side out, you need to shape the corners. Separate the front and back at one corner, centering the seam over the marked line to create a triangle. Measure from the tip of the triangle down the seam 1½" (3.6 cm), Draw a line perpendicular to the seam at that marking from fold to fold.

11. Stitch on the marked line, and backstitch at beginning and end of seam. Do not trim away triangle. Repeat for remaining three corners.

12. Turn the pillow cover right side out, and insert the pillow form.

13. Introduce your iPod to its new home slowly. It may not want to go, since it's used to being attached to your hip, but give it time and it will adapt to its new comfortable surroundings!

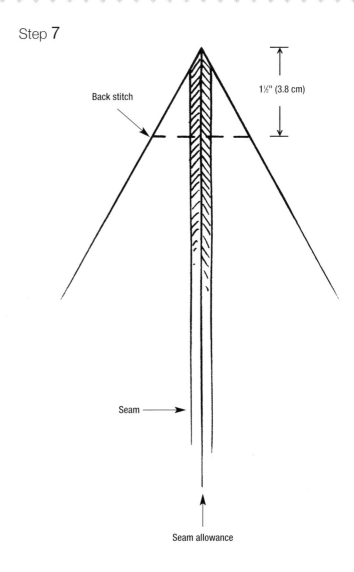

Step 7

Back stitch

1½" (3.8 cm)

Seam

Seam allowance

2

T-Shirt Quilt

A crew team celebrates victory.

When your T-shirt collection knows no limits, showcase those that mean the most.

Tools:

❀ Flat sheet
❀ Hand sewing needle
❀ Iron and ironing board
❀ Quilting pins
❀ Press cloth
❀ Sewing machine
❀ Scissors

Materials:

FOR A TWIN BED–SIZE QUILT:
52" x 78" (132.1 x 198.2 cm)

❀ 20 to 30 T-shirts (for quilt top)
❀ 2¼ yards (2 m) 54" (137.1 cm) -wide fusible tricot interfacing (for backing for T-shirts)
❀ 4½ yards (4.1 m) 54" (137.1 cm) shirting or ticking fabric (for quilt back)
❀ 2¼ yards (2 m) 54" (137.1 cm) -wide light-weight cotton batting
❀ 7½ yards (6.9 m) double-fold bias tape
❀ Thread

A former rower (and the project designer) fondly remembers the T-shirt challenge issued on the starting line of each boat race, announcing that the winning crew would be awarded the shirts from the losing crew. As an accomplished rower, he amassed a large collection of T-shirts from his competitive athletic days. They sat preciously folded in his closet. Squeezing into these treasured T-shirts was no longer an option (since his rowing weight was a thing of the past) and throwing them out would be heartbreaking, so a T-shirt quilt was an ingenious solution.

Everyone has his or her own stash of memorable T-shirts from rock concerts to varsity sports. Get them out of the closet and create a quilt full of memories, shaped by the colors and graphics of your own T-shirt collection. You can make the quilt any size, depending on how many T-shirts you have. This one fits a twin bed, but can be used as a throw on any size bed.

Instructions:

1. Prewash and dry the quilt back fabrics and bias tape to avoid shrinkage later.

2. Cut T-shirts into different shapes and sizes larger than 4" x 4" (10.2 x 10.2 cm). Keep cool looking logos and T-shirt patterns intact. You can also keep the whole front of some T-shirts.

3. Position all the T-shirt pieces on a flat sheet, folded to 52" x 78" (132.1 x 198.2 cm), to help you visualize the final product. Move, shift, and reshape the T-shirts until you like the pattern. It's kind of like a jigsaw puzzle.

4. Remove one shirt at a time and fuse interfacing to the wrong side, follow manufacturer's instructions. This strengthens the T-shirts and is especially important if they are old and worn.

5. Start in one corner, and sew the first two T-shirts together by laying one edge slightly over the adjoining edge and zigzag stitching over the visible cut edge with a narrow, dense zigzag stitch.

6. Continue to add and sew shirts to the first two. Be flexible; your plan will probably change as you sew.

7. Cut the quilt back fabric into two pieces, and the batting into one, all the same size, 53" x 79" (134.6 x 200.7 cm).

8. Create the quilt layers by placing the batting over one of the fabric back pieces and the T-shirt layer over the batting. Pin the layers together, starting in the center of the quilt and pinning out toward the edges.

9. Hand baste around the perimeter of the quilt.

10. Pin the bottom layer of the quilt to the other layers with the wrong sides together. Trim the edges and even up the corners. Hand baste around the edges through all layers.

11. Press open bias tape. Pin the open edge of the bias tape to the right side of the quilt with edges aligned. Fold back the starting end ½" (1.3 cm). Machine stitch in the bias tape crease nearest the edge. Continue sewing the bias tape until it overlaps at the beginning by ½" (1.3 cm).

12. Fold the bias tape to the back of the quilt, along the remaining crease, so that the folded edge reaches the stitching line and the bias tape encloses the raw edges.

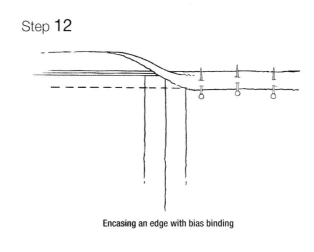

Step 12

Encasing an edge with bias binding

13. Edge stitch along the folded edge of the bias tape to secure and finish the quilt.

DIFFICULTY RATING

2

Goldfish Valance

Tools:

❀ Iron and ironing board
❀ Pins
❀ Press cloth
❀ Power drill or screwdriver
❀ Retractable metal tape measure
❀ Scissors
❀ Sewing machine
❀ Staple gun and staples

Materials:

❀ 1 yard (.9 m) 54" (137.1 cm) -wide white linen
❀ 1 yard (.9 m) muslin to cover mounting board
❀ Rubber stamp(s)
❀ Fabric ink pad, any color
❀ 1½" yards (3.8 cm) Self-Adhesive Velcro®
❀ ½" (1.3 cm) thick plywood, 5" to 7" (12.7 to 17.8 cm) wide; for length see step 2
❀ 2 (or more) L brackets, depending on length of mounting board
❀ Screws to fit L brackets

A crisp, linen valance is just the thing for a sun-drenched window.

Fact: Goldfish originated in China and are related to the common carp fish. They can live more than 20 years in optimal conditions; the world record is 49 years!

Mother Nature's popular shining underwater star

When I first met my boyfriend (who recently became my husband!), I was most endeared by his goldfish, Tallulah, that he kept in a bowl beside his bed. When he went to Costa Rica for a weeklong surfing trip, he asked me to take care of Tallulah. Conveniently, I was his neighbor, the girl next door. What are the chances of that happening in New York City? On my second day of goldfish duty, I couldn't get into his apartment. My key no longer turned the doorknob and all I could think about was Tallulah's little empty gold belly. Needless to say, when Joel came back, his beloved goldfish had not made it. Feeling incredibly guilt-ridden, I surprised him with a new google-eyed goldfish named Ceviche. (By the way, the lock was confirmed broken and I was off the hook.)

A goldfish is the inspiration for this linen valance. The designer drew a goldfish and had custom rubber stamps made. You can use a stock rubber stamp to make the project easier. This valance is 48" (111.8 cm) wide by 9" (22.9 cm) long, but make it any size to accommodate your window. Linen, with its semi-transparent qualities and inherent crispness, is an ideal fabric choice, perfect for any sun-drenched window.

Tip: Two brackets will support a short board, but use extra brackets if the board is long or the fabric is heavy.

Instructions:

1. Since every window is different, customize this project to fit your home.

2. Mark the location for the valance mounting board, 2" to 6" (5.1 to 15.2 cm) above the window frame and 4" (10.2 cm) beyond the window frame on each side. Measure the distance between the markings and cut the plywood accordingly.

   OPTIONAL: Cover the mounting board with muslin. Cut fabric large enough to wrap around all sides of the board. Center the board over the fabric and wrap the fabric to the top and staple it in place (much like wrapping a gift) If the fabric ravels, fold ½" (1.3 cm) to the wrong side and staple along the folded edge.

3. Attach L brackets 3" (7.6 cm) from each side onto the mounting board. Mark the bracket locations on the wall.

Step 3

MEASURE AND CUT FABRIC:

WIDTH: Length of board + 2 times the width of the board (return) + 3" (7.6 cm) hem allowance.

LENGTH: 12" (30.5 cm)

4. Press ¾" (1.9 cm) to the wrong side of all edges, press ¾" (1.9 cm) again. Edge stitch close to inside fold.

5. Apply the loop half of Velcro® to the mounting board on the three sides (not the side with the L brackets) that extend from the wall. Apply the soft side of the Velcro® to the top edge of the valance.

6. Choose a rubber stamp(s) or have a custom stamp made. The goldfish swimming on the valance pictured was drawn by the designer and made into a custom rubber stamp.

7. Practice stamping on scrap paper. Sometimes the edge of the stamp picks up extra ink and leaves a mark. If this happens, wipe the area clean with a baby wipe before each application.

8. Stamp the design randomly across the fabric valance.

9. Once the ink is dry, attach the valance to the mounting board with the Velcro. Hang the valance.

Aloha Picture Frames

Tools:

❀ Adhesive spray glue
❀ Butter knife
❀ Craft knife and cutting mat
❀ Double-sided tape
❀ Pencil
❀ Ruler
❀ Scissors

Materials:

❀ 3 different-size picture frames with precut photo mats (shadow box frames should be at least 1" [2.5 cm] deep)
❀ Remnants of Hawaiian print vintage fabric, slightly larger than photo mats
❀ 3 photographs
❀ Glazier's points
❀ Small piece of ¼" (6 mm) foam board (for shadow box option)

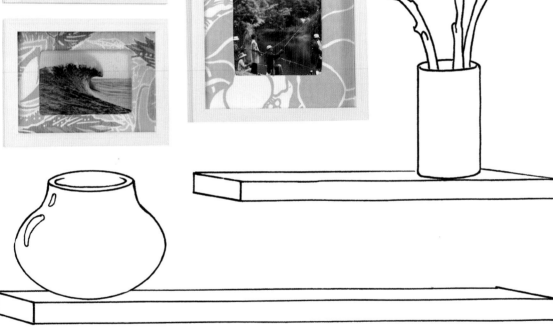

Bold Hawaiian fabrics brighten ordinary frames with island warmth and colorful energy.

Hawaii is the most perfect place in the world for my husband and me, and like most visitors, we often fantasize about living there one day. The islands of Hawaii are so seductive and intoxicating that we got married there and took our entire *ohana* with us for an extended vacation. Where else can you wear over-the-top aloha prints and walk barefoot with flowers in your hair? Hawaiian textiles reflect the vibrant colors in flower leis, fruits, fashion and the ocean, which are an integral part of Hawaiian culture.

Moved by the vintage fabrics of her *tutu's* (grandmother's) Hawaiian *mu'umu'us,* this designer created one-of-a-kind, shadow-box picture frames.

The designer's photographs (her girlfriends on the beach, fisherman on the Big Island, and a wave pounding the south shore of Kauai) are images from Hawaii that she keeps with her to remind her of home, while she is on the mainland.

Hawaiian foliage reflects the vibrant colors that are Hawaii.

Instructions:

1. Choose a photograph that fits the mat and frame, and fabric that works with the photo.

2. Cut fabric 1" (2.6 cm) longer and wider than the frame.

3. Center the mat on the wrong side of the fabric and trace the mat opening with a pencil. Use the ruler to draw cutting lines ½" (1.3 cm) inside the mat opening markings.

4. Cut the opening for the photograph along the inside cutting lines.

5. Carefully, cut a diagonal slit at each corner up to the original mat opening marking. This helps you fold the fabric over the mat neatly.

6. Place the fabric face down on a flat surface. Spray adhesive on the fabric and center the mat along the inside markings and ½" (1.3 cm) from the outside edge.

7. Fold the fabric edges to the back of the mat along the inside and outer edges, so the mat is completely covered with fabric and the corners are smooth. If necessary, add more adhesive to hold the edges to the back of the mat.

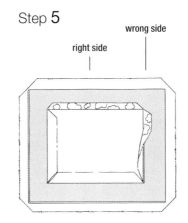

Step 5

wrong side

right side

8. Use double-sided tape to hold the photograph behind the mat and to the backing cardboard included with the frame.

9. Close the frame, or if you want to make a shadow box, continue with the next steps.

TO MAKE A SHADOW BOX:

1. Remove the clamps that hold the frame closed.

2. Use a craft knife to cut ½" (1.3 cm) by ¼" (6 mm) rectangular pieces of foam board, 2 pieces for each corner.

3. Place the glass in the frame.

4. Using double-sided tape, stick the foam pieces at right angles inside the corners of the frame, so they are flush to the edges of the frame and invisible from the right side.

5. Lay the fabric-covered mat and photograph on top of the foam board corners.

6. Use the back of a butter knife to insert glazier's points into the center of each side of the frame to hold it closed.

7. Hang the frames on the wall in a cluster.

8. Buy some orchids and pretend you're back on the Big Island.

Pompon Party Napkins

Pompons add a feeling of festivity wherever you attach them.

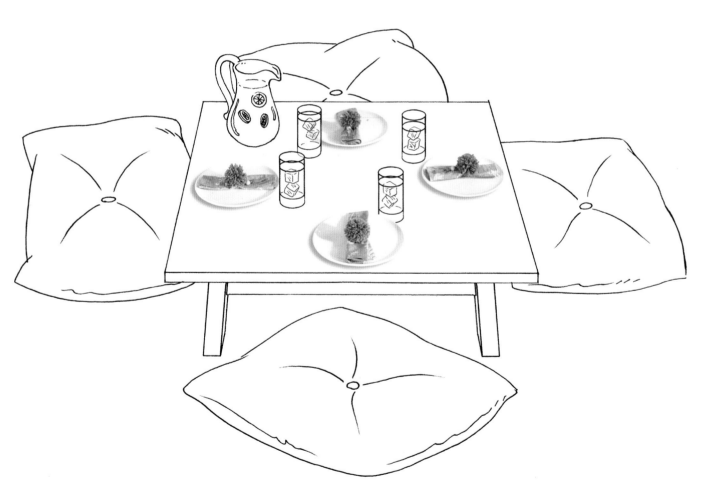

I was browsing through the home section of an upscale department store, when some elegantly displayed cloth napkins caught my eye. At $29 (£15), each you could say they were on the pricey side; coincidentally I had the exact same fabric at home! Well, a little craftiness is good for the wallet. I made a set of four napkins with neatly mitered corners for under $10 (£5) in no time. I even improved on the retail napkins by making pompons resembling whimsical flowers, to act as napkin holders. Do you remember when pom-pons were kind of cool? When I was a child, they were everywhere: on ice skates, on sweater ties, and on crazy winter hats; and I used to make pompons animals with googly eyes! Resurrect this fun decoration as a chic table accessory.

Pompons on my ice skates

Fact: Is it Pompon or Pom-Pom? Pompons by defintion are decorative balls of fluff that come in many colors, and sizes, and are made from a wide array of materials, including fabric, plastic, and even feathers. In cheerleading, they are used in pairs. However, when speaking about clothing or decorative uses, the spelling *pom-pom* is equally common and also considered correct.

Tools:

* Compass
* Disappearing-ink fabric pen
* Iron and ironing board
* Scissors
* Sewing machine
* Yardstick

Materials:

FOR 4 NAPKINS:
20" x 20" (50.8 x 50.8 cm)

* 1¼ yards (1.25 m) 45" (114.3 cm) -wide fabric
* Matching thread

FOR 4 POM PONS:

* Knitting worsted yarn
* Four ⅝" (1.6 cm) -diameter wooden beads
* 8" x 10" (20.3 x 25.4 cm) piece of cardboard

Instructions:

NAPKIN INSTRUCTIONS:

1. Cut four squares of fabric 22½" x 22½" (57.2 x 57.2 cm).

2. Sew a straight stitch ¼" (6 mm) from the edge on all sides, press the raw edge to the wrong side along the stitching and stitch it in place.

3. To form a miter at the corners, press the remaining 1" (2.5 cm) hem allowance to the wrong side on all sides. (see How to Form a Mitered Corner, page 145)

4. Topstitch the hem.

POMPON INSTRUCTIONS:
3½" (8.9 cm)

1. Use the compass to draw two 4" (10.2 cm) -diameter circles each with a 1.5" (3.8 cm) -diameter circle in the center. Draw two parallel lines from the inner circles to the outer circles. Cut out the outer circle along the parallel lines and the inner circle to create 2 cardboard templates.

Step 1

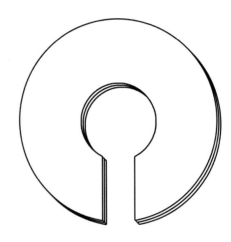

Cardboard templates

2. Hold the two pieces of cardboard together and wind the yarn evenly around the ring until you reach the desired fullness. (about 100 wraps). Cut the yarn around the outside edge, between the two pieces of cardboard.

Step 2

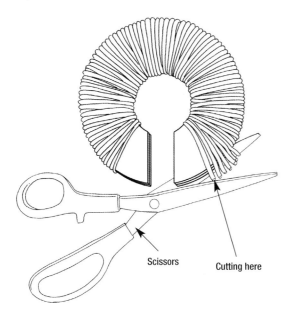

Scissors   Cutting here

Yarn wrapped around template

3. Cut three pieces of yarn 12" (30.5 cm) long and wrap them between the two pieces of cardboard around the center of the cut yarn.

4. Tie the three pieces of yarn into a slip knot and tighten it as much as possible. Secure with an additional knot. Remove the cardboard pieces.

Step 5

3 strands of yarn layering over template

5. Braid three tie yarns together to create two braided strands.

6. When the strands are 5" (12.7 cm) long, braid both strands together to form a single, larger braid.

7. Slip on a natural wood bead. If the yarn ends make it hard to get the bead on, wet and twist them. Knot the yarn below the bead.

FURTHER INSTRUCTIONS:

1. Lay a folded napkin on the braided loop. Bring the pompon and bead together, slipping the pompon through the braided loop. Voilà, it's time for tea sandwiches and coffee in the garden.

Stitch and Technique Glossary

Slip Stitch

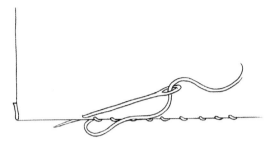

Used to join two finished edges. Insert the needle inside the folded fabric edge and bring it out through the folded edge about ¼" (6 mm) away. Then insert the needle into the fold of the opposite edge and form the same stitch. Repeat, alternating from side to side with each stitch.

Straight Stitch

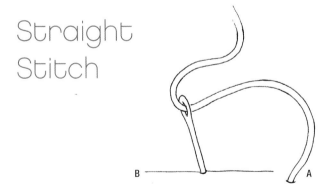

Individual stitches used alone or to form a straight line. Bring the needle up from wrong side of the fabric (A) and then back down the desired length away (B). Repeat as needed.

Running Stitch

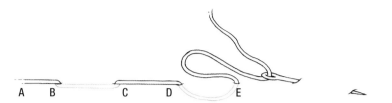

Strong enough to use for seams. Bring the needle up from the wrong side of the fabric (A). Then, insert the point of the needle in, (B) and then out (C) of the fabric several times (D, E) before pulling the thread through. Keep the stitches and the spaces between them small and even.

Satin Stitch

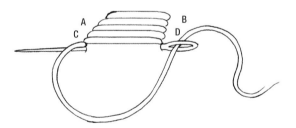

A filling stitch, used to add color and pattern. Outline the design area with a disappearing ink fabric pen. Bring the needle up from the wrong side along one end of the marking (A). Carry the thread across the design to the opposite marking (B) and insert the needle. Slide the needle under the fabric, so it emerges on the opposite side (C). Carry the thread across the design again, next to the first stitch and insert the needle (D). Continue, keeping stitches close together and flat.

Back Stitch

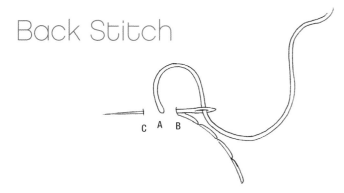

A strong stitch used to outline an area. Bring the needle up from the wrong side of the fabric **(A)** and then, insert it ⅛" (3 mm) behind the point where it came out of the fabric **(B)**. Then, insert it the same distance, ⅛" (3 mm) in front of the point where it came out of the fabric **(C)**. Repeat.

Lazy Daisy Stitch

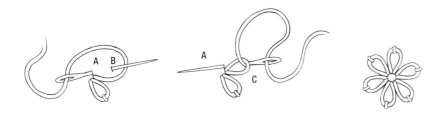

This stitch can be individual or grouped. Bring the needle up from the wrong side of the fabric **(A)**. Hold the thread to form a loop. Insert the needle near the spot where the thread emerged from the wrong side **(A)** and, then bring it up a short distance below to form a loop **(B)**. Reinsert the needle to make a small stitch over the end of the loop **(C)** and bring the needle back to the right side near **(A)** again to form a circle of loops.

Chain Stitch

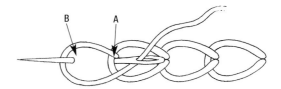

This is a linked series of lazy daisy stitches, used to create a border or to fill an area. Make one lazy daisy stitch, but do not pull the thread taut. Instead of taking the small stitch over the end of the loop, make the next stitch by inserting the needle inside the loop at the place where the thread emerged to form the first stitch **(A)**, and then back out **(B)** to from the same size loop. Repeat, keeping stitches the same size.

Cross Stitch

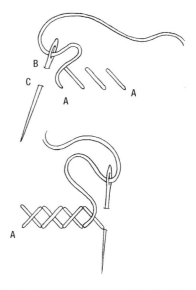

A decorative stitch done in two in separate rows of single, diagonal stitches. Bring the needle up from the wrong side **(A)** at the lower right side of the area to be stitched. Insert the needle above and to the left **(B)** and bring it out below at point **(C)**. Continue making single, slanting stitches by keeping the needle vertical. Once you have completed the row, work back from left to right by making a second row of diagonal stitches that cross over the first. Insert the needle at the ends of the stitches in the first row. Mark parallel lines with a disappearing-ink fabric pen to help keep the stitches the same length.

Stitch in the Ditch

Sew a regular seam and press the seam allowances open. From the right side, machine stitch directly over the previous stitching.

Slip Knot

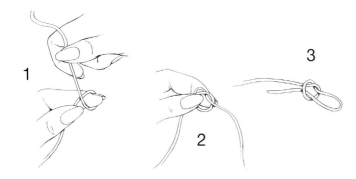

1

2

3

Wrap the yarn around your left forefinger. Slide the loop off your finger and pass the yarn behind it so it looks like a pretzel. Pull the yarn, visible in the center of the loop through the loop without letting the end through. This forms a slip knot that you can tighten and loosen.

How to Draw a Circle

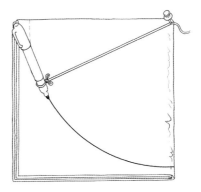

Fold your fabric into quarters. Tie a piece of string around a disappearing-ink fabric pen and cut the string so the length from the pen to the end of the string equals the radius of the circle you wish to draw. Pin the loose end of the string to the folded corner. Hold the pen upright, and with the string taut; draw the curve from fabric side to side. Cut along the marking through all fabric layers.

How to Staple a Corner Fold

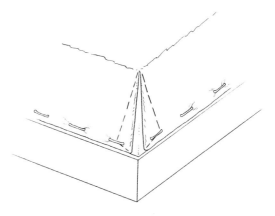

Staple the fabric to each side almost to the corners. Fold each corner edge into a triangular inverted pleat and staple it near the corner. Trim excess fabric.

How to Form a Mitered Corner

Step 1

Finish the raw edge and press the hem to the wrong side.

Step 2

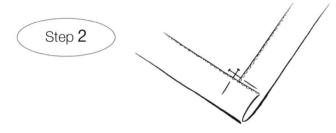

Place a pin on each side perpendicularly through the hem at the point where the two hems intersect.

Step 3

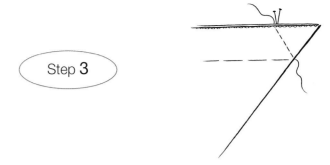

Unfold the hem and with right sides together, align the finished edges to form a diagonal fold, matching the pins. Draw a line between the point where the two hem creases and the pins intersect and stitch over the guideline. Backstitch at the beginning and end of the seam. Trim off the corner.

Step 4

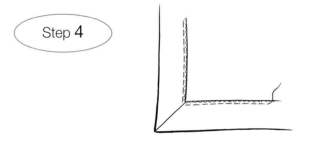

Finger press the seam allowances open and turn the corner to the inside and press. Topstitch next to the inside fold.

How to Use a Grid to Copy a Design

The pattern or design you want to copy will appear on a grid. Draw a new grid the indicated size (1" [2.5 cm], 2" [5.1 cm], etc) on a large piece of craft paper. You might need a yardstick. Copy the design or pattern from the first grid, square by square by duplicating it on the new, larger grid. You can reduce the size of a design with the same method, by drawing a smaller grid.

Resources

Retail Resources:

Bocage
www.bocagenewyork.com
antique buttons, craft supplies

Fabric.com
888.455.2940
www.fabric.com
fabrics (linen, burlap, silks), trims, craft supplies

Hancock Fabrics
www.hancockfabrics.com
fabrics, trims

Home Depot
www.homedepot.com
precut acrylic, cabinet hardware

Marimekko® Corporation (USA)
Textile Arts
PO Box 3151
Sag Harbor, NY 11963 USA
888.343.7285
631.725.1714
info@txtlart.com
patterned fabrics, oilcloth

Marimekko Corporation
Puusepänkatu 4
00880 Helsinki, Finland
P.O. Box 107, 00811 Helsinki, Finland
Tel. +358.9.758.71
Fax +358.9.755.3051
www.marimekko.fi
patterned fabrics, oilcloth

Michaels
The Arts and Crafts Store®
800.MICHAELS
www.michaels.com
arts and craft supplies

Pearl™
The World's Largest Discount Art Supplier
800.451.7327
www.pearlpaint.com
prestretched art canvas, arts and craft supplies

Reprodepot Fabrics
877.738.7632
custserv@reprodepot.com
www.reprodepot.com
fabrics, trims, appliqués, gifts

Waverly®
www.waverly.com
fabrics

www.fleamarketguide.com
State-by-state flea market listings in United States

www.discoverfrance.net/France/Paris/Shopping/
Paris_fleamkts2.shtml
Paris flea markets and antique dealers

Trade Resources:

F. Schumacher & Co.
79 Madison Avenue
New York, NY 10016 USA
800.523.1200
www.fschumacher.com
fabrics

Knoll International Textiles
76 Ninth Avenue, 11th floor
New York, NY 10011 USA
866.565.5858
www.knoll.com
fabrics

Vitra, Inc.
29 Ninth Avenue
New York, NY 10014 USA
212.463.5700
www.vitra.com

Zimmer + Rohde (USA)
Decoration & Design Building
979 Third Avenue, Suite 1616
New York, NY 10022 USA
212.758.5357
fabrics

Zimmer+Rohde
Zimmersmuhlenweg 14–16
61440 Oberurse
Frankfurt, Germany
www.zimmer-rohde.com
fabrics

About the Author

Cat Wei is an architect, interior designer, television host, design consultant, and an inspiringly creative person, with a full résumé of design-related jobs and projects. After receiving her Bachelor's of Environmental Design degree from the University of Colorado at Boulder, Cat moved back to the northeast, and into New York City to earn her Master's of Architecture degree from Columbia University. While in graduate school, Cat worked for such high-profile firms as Agrest and Gandelsonas, and Skidmore, Owings, and Merrill. Upon graduation, Cat honed her interior design skills at several boutique design firms, including UT (a.k.a. Richardson Sakeki), the firm that is best know for the Bliss and Skinklinic spas. Cat kept attuned to the architecture world, by teaching architecture studio at the New York Institute of Technology. In January 2004, Cat joined the cast of *Trading Spaces Family* as a designer, and recently finished filming *She's Moving In* for the WE Network. As cohost of *Material Girls on the Do-It-Yourself Network*, Cat showcases her craftiness as a member of the "seam team" by demonstrating to the homeowner and the viewers how to completely transform a home, using fabric. Cat lives in New York City with her husband, Joel, and her miniature dachshund, Duke.

Contributing Designers

Matt Albiani a New England–raised, New York–based fashion photographer, former rower, lover of all things creative, divides his time between New York City and Montauk, Long Island. **www.exposureny.com**

Stephanie Kheder Bodine has a passion for designing her own version of anything and everything to make life more exciting! Influenced by funky fashions, furnishings, ornamentation, and her experiences of living in New York City, this Midwestern girl broke out and took her collectible and art obsession to the next level. Best known for her notions boutique, Bocage **(www.bocage newyork.com)**, Stephanie has developed a loyal following. She has become a favorite resource for unusual and sophisticated inspiration, knowledge, and embellishing details for oneself and one's surroundings.

Janessa Bautista is the founder of her company, a fortes design, based in New York City. As a clothing and textile designer, she aspires to create a line of products that is beautiful and functional. Her clothing line is simple and modest and was her first step into building a collection of various products that incorporate her handmade textiles. All of her products are created locally and she customizes her textiles by silk-screening each design, making every piece unique. **www.fortesdesign.com**

Sheila Brennan is a designer, and has been working in Paris, France, for the past five years. Previously, she worked in the fashion industry in New York, London and Paris. Most recently, Sheila she has been interested in soft furnishing design, inspired by her clothing pattern-making skills. She likes to incorporate tailored finishing details and luxury suiting fabrics to make cushions and other fabric-based home furnishings. Sheila was born in New York, and studied fashion design in Ireland.

Meleana Blaich moved from her home in Hawaii to New York City to start a handbag company, and she is currently designing her first clothing collection. Inspiration for her handbags comes from her Hawaiian culture, primarily the fabrics of old Hawaii. The bright floral prints that are the focus of her handbag collection are vintage pieces that she has collected from Hawaii and throughout her travels. Meleana's current clothing collection, although more contemporary in style, does include touches of Hawaiian textiles. Her handbags are sold in small boutiques around the country and on her Web site. **www.meleana.com**

Prim Cheunsumran is an art director living and working in New York.

Trudy Dinnhaupt is a professional seamstress, residing in Knoxville, Tennessee. With thirty years of sewing experience, she has worked on a wide variety of projects from sewing and designing her own wedding dress, to carnival ride seats, to designer dog wear, to every home décor item imaginable. She is also the head seamstress for Do-It-Yourself network's *Material Girls*. KMDECHO@aol.com

Gigi Guerra is a writer and editor for *Lucky Magazine*. She graduated from Parsons School of Design with a degree in fashion design. gigi_guerra@yahoo.com

Jenny Harada was schooled in the disciplines of graphic design and toy design. Consequently, when she became a grown up, she chose animation as her career. Seven years later, she got married to an awesome tattoo artist named Mark, had a sweet baby named Lukas, and stopped animating. That's when she seriously started making stuffed toys. Her ideas come from daydreams and nightmares that never cease to taunt her. She owes her sewing skill to her mother, who started teaching her at the wee age of seven. Jenny also likes to paint and to grow things in her garden. She hopes one day to have her very own tree farm. Jenny was born and raised in New York, and she and her family now reside in Ohio. www.jennyharada.com

Eugenie Huang studied at the Massachusetts Institute of Technology and the Columbia Graduate School of Architecture. She shares a cooperative architectural practice, Formactiv Architecture, Design and Technology PC, founded in 2000 with Ron Eng and collaborators. Her current endeavors include the examination of wearable jewelry informed by architectural concepts. **www.formactiv.net**

Jocelyn Joson cofounded Mad Mad Judy after working for many years as a stylist and designer for the Martha Stewart empire. Her skills in all forms of handicraft are now primarily manifested in a line of one-of-a-kind jewelry and accessories. Jocelyn fashions her creations by reworking vintage pieces with modern materials, using various forms of knotting, crocheting, knitting, and sewing. **www.madmadjudy.co**

Tana Lauritsen and Mike Cieciora are the founders of **ponyBeaver.com**, a design company specializing in handmade items such as T-shirts, pillows, pet scarves, and home décor. Tana is a graphic designer and Mike is a writer and a painter. They live together in Brooklyn. **www.ponybeaver.com**

Ginny Mavroleon began her fashion career with Vicky Tiel and Valentino in Paris, and then moved to New York to work with Joia, Kenzo, and Paul Smith. In the late 1980s, she moved to her beach house and began to combine nature with fashion. Mavroleon's diverse talents incorporate her love of color and texture into home accessories and clothing.Vibrant hand-painted serving trays inlaid with home grown flowers, indigenous leaves mounted and framed into botanical prints, and a unique line of soft silk clothing infused with Swarovski crystals are her signature pieces. A native of the United Kingdom, Ginny Mavroleon resides on the East End of Long Island with her two sons. **blaklion@optonline.net**

Patrick Saint Jean is an aspiring fashion designer. He currently resides in New York City where his upcoming clothing line will be based.
saintjeans@yahoo.com

Jessica Smith has a bachelor of fine arts in painting from the University of Washington and a master's of fine arts in textile design from the University of Kansas. In her studio, Smith produces a limited edition line of home textiles and bags, called Domestic Element. She continually explores different techniques for creating patterns that merge historical motifs with contemporary conversation. Smith's work has been published in the magazines *Fiberarts* and *American Craft*, to name a few. Her work is exhibited across the country, most recently at the Copper Hewitt Triennial, Museum Design Atlanta, School of Visual Arts West Side Gallery in New York, and Woven Fiber Art House in West Chester, Pennsylvania. Presently, Smith lives in Seattle, Washington. **www.domesticelement.com**

Jane Wei is Cat's mom, and sewer extraordinaire. She is responsible for the fabulous outfits Cat wore as a child. Jane is a real estate agent who lives with Cat's dad, a retired doctor. They reside in Westchester County, New York.

Kelly Wilson grew up in a family of talented craftspeople. She enjoys experimenting with various materials and playing with different techniques to create knit and crochet pieces that are fabulously fun. More of her designs can be found at **www.kellywilsondesigns.com**, **www.anastasi aknits.com**, and **www.theknitting-vault.com**. She has coauthored two books for Quarry Books: *The Knitter's Guide to Yarn Cocktails* and *The Crocheter's Guide to Yarn Cocktails*. Look for Kelly in episodes of Do-It-Yourself network's *Knitty Gritty* show, where she demonstrates how to make her designs for car accessories and jewelry.

Katherine Wong grew up dividing her time between Hong Kong and Vancouver. She studied architecture at the Rhode Island School of Design. Currently, she works in an architecture firm in NYC. **katherinewong@gmail.com**

Leyden Yaeger After graduating from the masters of architecture program at Columbia University in 1997, Leyden worked at several architecture, design and branding firms in New York City. In 2001, she moved to Los Angeles to pursue modern architecture and its relationship to nature and site. In 2006, Leyden joined the design team at Shook Kelley, a renowned branding and perception design firm located in North Carolina and Los Angeles. Leyden's specialties include residential architecture and interiors, retail and restaurant design, and brand identity. **Leyden@shookkelley.com**

Acknowledgments

Thank you to all the designers who helped give this book variety and spice!

Special thanks to:
Quarry Books: Betsy Gammons, Winnie Prentiss, Regina Grenier, Cora Hawks, and Candice Janco

Photographers Miki Iwamura, Susan Pittard, Jack Parker, Allan Penn, and the team at Creative Publishing international

DIY Network and Rivr Media for creating *Material Girls* and the amazing cast and crew of *Material Girls*

My agents Mark Turner and Maura Teitelbaum at Abrams Artists Agency

Patrick Saint Jean for his sewing expertise

fabric.com, txtlart.com, reprodepot.com, Vitra, Waverly, Zimmer+Rohde

My husband Joel

My brother Jim

Duke the dachshund

Old friends and new family

Photographer Credits

Project photography by Allan Penn and Creative Publishing international

All inspiration shots from www.istock.com, with the exception of the following:

Matt Albiani, 132 (right)
Stephanie Bodine, 33
Prim Chuensumran, 49
Miki Iwaruma, 92 (right)
Courtesy of Marimekko/www.marimekko.com,105
Susan Pittard, 147
Eric Roth, 19 (left)
Courtesy of www.vitra.com, 126
Catherine Wei, 23
www.fotofolia.com, 115

PROJECT CREDITS

Ruched Lace Lampshade

Page 26

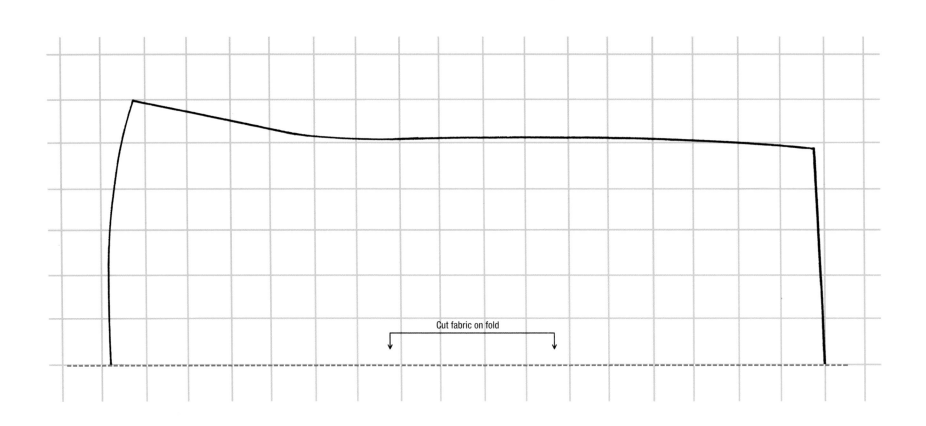

Cut fabric on fold

Half pattern for ruched lampshade panel

Patchwork Taxidermy Rug

Page 28

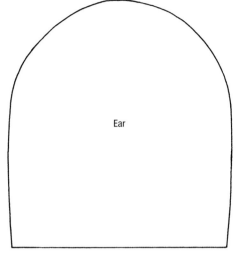 Photo copy at 300%

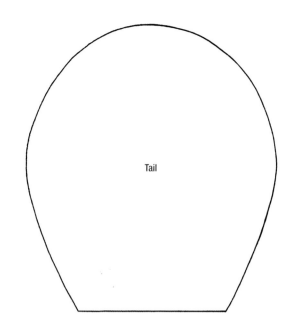

Ear

Tail

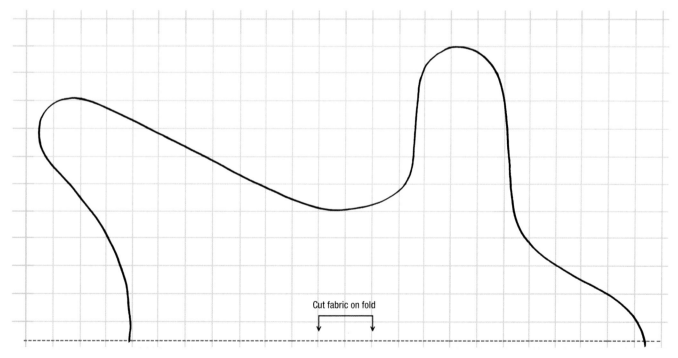

Cut fabric on fold

Half pattern for rug

Water Lily Table Runner

Page 48

Photo copy at 150%

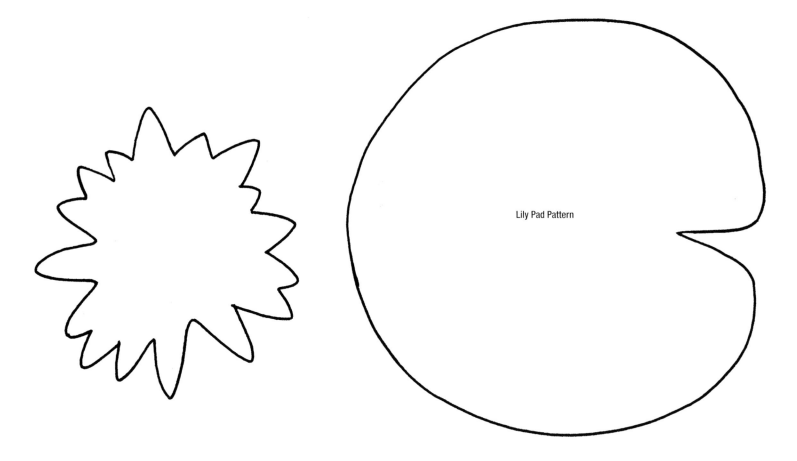

Lily Pad Pattern

Heartfelt Toaster Cozy

Page 84

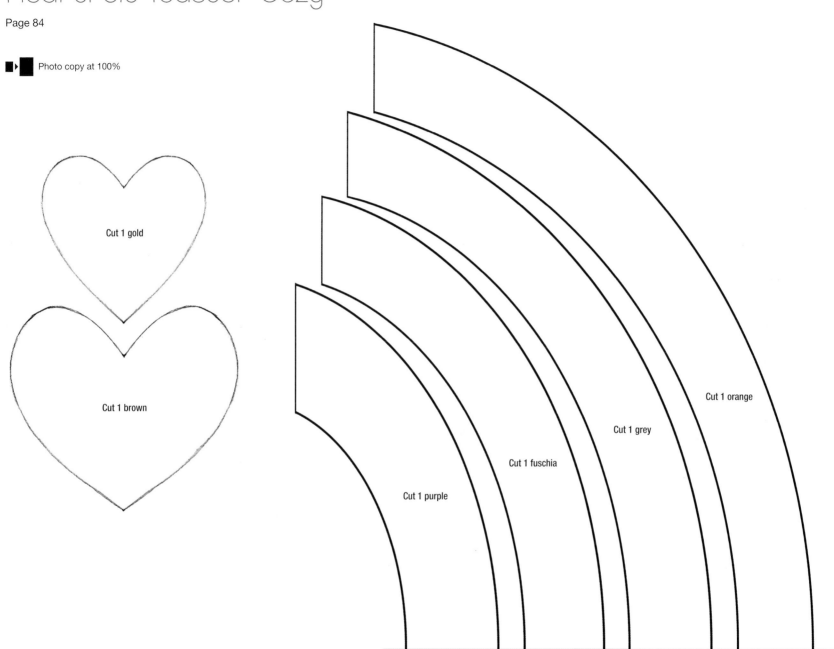

Photo copy at 100%

Cut 1 gold

Cut 1 brown

Cut 1 purple

Cut 1 fuschia

Cut 1 grey

Cut 1 orange

Mod-ern Tasseled Shade

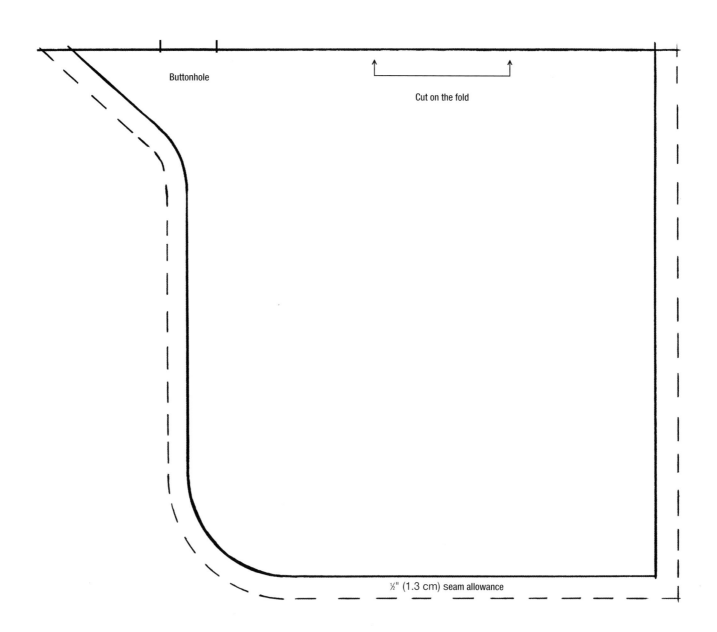

Photo copy at 200%

Buttonhole

Cut on the fold

½" (1.3 cm) seam allowance

Antler Trophy Pillow

Page 116

Photo copy at 200%

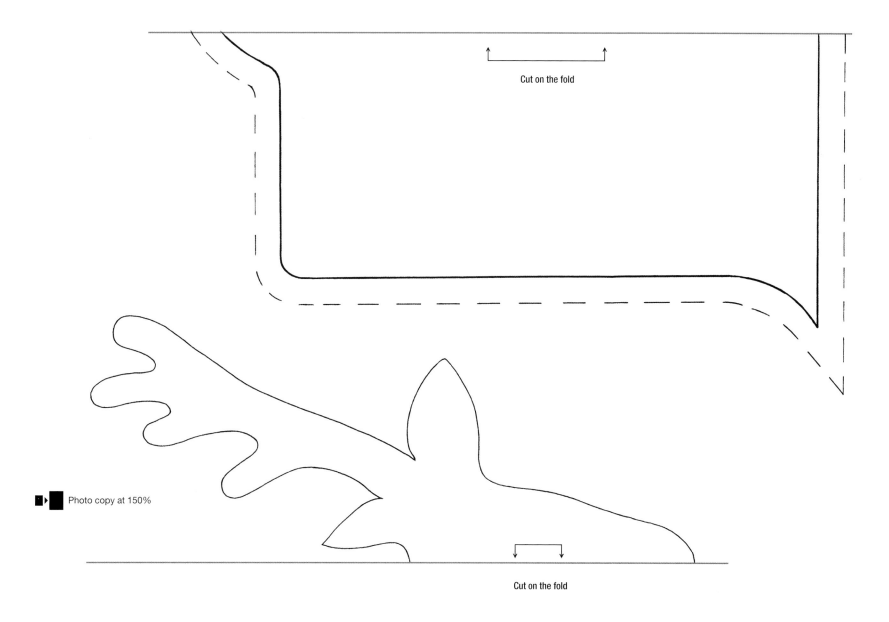

Cut on the fold

Photo copy at 150%

Cut on the fold

Fancy Plants Chair

Page 76

Photo copy at 300%

Tromp l'Oeil Pendant Lamp

Page 124

Photo copy at 100%

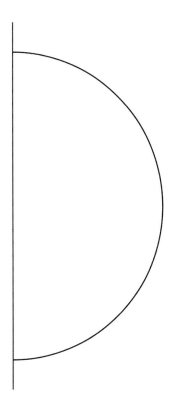